ClearRevise®

BTEC Tech Award Level 1/2 in **Sport**

Illustrated revision and practice

Component 3:
Developing fitness to improve performance

Published by
PG Online Limited
The Old Coach House
35 Main Road
Tolpuddle
Dorset
DT2 7EW
United Kingdom

sales@pgonline.co.uk
www.pgonline.co.uk
2024

PG ONLINE

PREFACE

Absolute clarity! That's the aim.

This is everything you need to ace the examined component in this course and beam with pride. Each topic is laid out in a beautifully illustrated format that is clear, approachable and as concise and simple as possible.

Each section of the PE specification is clearly indicated to help you cross-reference your revision. The checklist on the contents pages will help you keep track of what you have already worked through and what's left before the big day.

We have included worked exam-style questions with answers for almost every topic. This helps you understand where marks are coming from and to see the theory at work for yourself in an exam situation. There is also a set of exam-style questions at the end of each topic for you to practise writing answers for. You can check your answers against those given at the end of the book.

LEVELS OF LEARNING

Based on the degree to which you are able to truly understand a new topic, we recommend that you work in stages. Start by reading a short explanation of something, then try and recall what you've just read. This has limited effect if you stop there but it aids the next stage. Question everything. Write down your own summary and then complete and mark a related exam-style question. Cover up the answers if necessary but learn from them once you've seen them. Lastly, teach someone else. Explain the topic in a way that they can understand. Have a go at the different practice questions – they offer an insight into how and where marks are awarded.

ACKNOWLEDGMENTS

Every effort has been made to trace and acknowledge ownership of copyright. The publishers will be happy to make any future amendments with copyright owners that it has not been possible to contact. The publisher would like to thank the following companies and individuals who granted permission for the use of their images in this textbook.

Javelin thrower © EvrenKalinbacak / Shutterstock
HSBC World Rugby match © Mai Groves / Shutterstock
London Marathon runners © IR Stone / Shutterstock
Event rider © Anthony Delgado / Shutterstock
Boxing match © Dmitry Niko / Shutterstock
All other photographs and graphics © Shutterstock.

Design and artwork: Simon Hartshorne & Jessica Webb / PG Online Ltd
First edition 2024 10 9 8 7 6 5 4 3 2 1
A catalogue entry for this book is available from the British Library
ISBN: 978-1-916518-08-7

This product is made of material from well-managed FSC®-certified forests and recycled materials.
Printed by Bell and Bain Ltd, Glasgow, UK.

MIX
Paper | Supporting responsible forestry
FSC® C007785

THE SCIENCE OF REVISION

Illustrations and words

Research has shown that revising with words and pictures doubles the quality of responses by students.[1] This is known as 'dual-coding' because it provides two ways of fetching the information from our brain. The improvement in responses is particularly apparent in students when they are asked to apply their knowledge to different problems. Recall, application and judgement are all specifically and carefully assessed in public examination questions.

Retrieval of information

Retrieval practice encourages students to come up with answers to questions.[2] The closer the question is to one you might see in a real examination, the better. Also, the closer the environment in which a student revises is to the 'examination environment', the better. Students who had a test 2–7 days away did 30% better using retrieval practice than students who simply read, or repeatedly reread material. Students who were expected to teach the content to someone else after their revision period did better still.[3] What was found to be most interesting in other studies is that students using retrieval methods and testing for revision were also more resilient to the introduction of stress.[4]

Ebbinghaus' forgetting curve and spaced learning

Ebbinghaus' 140-year-old study examined the rate at which we forget things over time. The findings still hold true. However, the act of forgetting facts and techniques and relearning them is what cements them into the brain.[5] Spacing out revision is more effective than cramming – we know that, but students should also know that the space between revisiting material should vary depending on how far away the examination is. A cyclical approach is required. An examination 12 months away necessitates revisiting covered material about once a month. A test in 30 days should have topics revisited every 3 days – intervals of roughly a tenth of the time available.[6]

Summary

Students: the more tests and past questions you do, in an environment as close to examination conditions as possible, the better you are likely to perform on the day. If you prefer to listen to music while you revise, tunes without lyrics will be far less detrimental to your memory and retention. Silence is most effective.[5] If you choose to study with friends, choose carefully – effort is contagious.[7]

1. Mayer, R. E., & Anderson, R. B. (1991). Animations need narrations: An experimental test of dual-coding hypothesis. *Journal of Education Psychology*, (83)4, 484–490.

2. Roediger III, H. L., & Karpicke, J.D. (2006). Test-enhanced learning: Taking memory tests improves long-term retention. *Psychological Science*, 17(3), 249–255.

3. Nestojko, J., Bui, D., Kornell, N. & Bjork, E. (2014). Expecting to teach enhances learning and organisation of knowledge in free recall of text passages. *Memory and Cognition*, 42(7), 1038–1048.

4. Smith, A. M., Floerke, V. A., & Thomas, A. K. (2016) Retrieval practice protects memory against acute stress. *Science*, 354(6315), 1046–1048.

5. Perham, N., & Currie, H. (2014). Does listening to preferred music improve comprehension performance? *Applied Cognitive Psychology*, 28(2), 279–284.

6. Cepeda, N. J., Vul, E., Rohrer, D., Wixted, J. T. & Pashler, H. (2008). Spacing effects in learning a temporal ridgeline of optimal retention. *Psychological Science*, 19(11), 1095–1102.

7. Busch, B. & Watson, E. (2019), *The Science of Learning*, 1st ed. Routledge.

CONTENTS AND CHECKLIST

Topic A Explore the importance of fitness for sports performance

Topic B Investigate fitness testing to determine fitness levels

Topic C Investigate different fitness training methods

Topic D Investigate fitness programming to improve fitness and sports performance

MARK ALLOCATIONS

Green mark allocations[1] on answers to in-text questions throughout this guide help to indicate where marks are gained within the answers. A bracketed '1' e.g. [1] = one valid point worthy of a mark.

In longer answer questions, a mark is given based on the whole response. In these answers, a tick mark [✓] indicates that a valid point has been made. For a mark, a judgement should be made using the levels-based mark scheme on **page 59**.

There are often many more points to make than there are marks available so you have more opportunity to max out your answers than you may think.

COMMAND VERBS

The exam paper that you take will use the following command verbs in each question. You may understand lots about a topic, but if you do not answer each question in the correct way, the mark you get may be very low.

Study each of the below command verbs along with their meanings and how they are used to answer a question.

Give

Recall one or more pieces of information. These are short answers with 1 mark for each point.

Give **two** benefits of a warm up [2]

To increase body temperature,[1] and increase the range of movement.[1]

State or name

Recall facts, terms or processes, or provide the correct answer to the given context.

Name **one** type of technology Jo can use to measure exercise intensity. [1]

Smartwatch with a heart rate monitor built in.[1]

Complete

Provide some missing information for a given table or diagram.

Adnan is looking to start regular fitness training with a local provider. Complete **Table 1** by naming **two** types of provision. [2]

	Type of provision
(i)	Private [1]
(ii)	Voluntary [1]

Table 1

Draw

Match one option to a choice of five possible answers.

Draw a straight line to match the test method to the correct component of fitness. [1]

Vertical jump test — Power[1]

Agility
Balance
Coordination
Power[1]
Reaction time

Describe

Present two (or more) linked descriptive points on characteristics, features, uses or processes. You do not need to include a justification or reason.

Describe what is meant by intrinsic motivation. [2]

Intrinsic motivation comes from within the performer.[1] They may want to feel a sense of accomplishment, pride or satisfaction.[1]

Identify

Identify the correct answer from the given context.

Identify the fitness test being performed in **Figure 2**.

Sit and reach test.[1]

Explain

An explain question needs two parts. First give a reason and then give a linked explanation of why this example answers the question. Make sure to use words such as 'because' or 'so' in this type of question.

Andy has been asked to complete a PAR-Q assessment before starting a training programme.

Explain **one** reason a PAR-Q assessment is necessary. [2]

A PAR-Q assessment outlines any existing health issues[1] so a safe programme can be put together for him.[1]

Reason

Linked explanation

Assess

Identify the problem or issue in the question.

Explore the relevant points that relate to the problem or issue with logical thoughts or arguments.

Think how they interrelate.

Links to content within either Component 1 or 2 can be expected in these questions.

You should use full paragraphs to answer these questions with a supporting judgement where appropriate.

The full answer will usually be about a page of writing.

Melanie is hoping to start a new exercise programme to improve her health.

Assess how frequency, intensity, time and type (FITT) can be applied to a healthy training programme. [6]

Training needs to happen regularly but leave time to rest and recover. Intensity, such as the incline, resistance or weights needs to challenge the performer without excessive strain. The time or length of each training session will also impact on the intensity and the recovery period. The type of training needs to be linked to the performance goals of the individual and be varied to improve motivation. Variation of activity also allows one muscle group to rest while another is being worked.

Accurate and relevant knowledge

Detailed knowledge

Clear links between points

Relevant to the question context

Evaluate

1) Write down all the factors or events that apply to a given context.
2) Consider the strengths and weaknesses of each.
3) Identify those that are most important.
4) Give a reasoned conclusion supported by evidence.

Links to content within either Component 1 or 2 will be expected in these questions.

You should use full paragraphs to answer these questions.

The full answer will usually be about a page of text.

A coach at a seaside water sports centre wants to test the components of skills-related fitness of its top performers.

They are considering using the stork stand test and the vertical jump test.

Evaluate the effectiveness of the stork stand test and the vertical jump test for determining the performance of surfers and kayakers. [6]

Both surfing and kayaking involve balance and power but kayakers *have a much lower centre of gravity when seated and a paddle to help steady them. They also don't use their legs as much as surfers.* Therefore, a kayaker is unlikely to require balance as much as a surfer who needs to be able to stand on a board without a paddle.

- Accurate and relevant factor
- *Importance of the factor*
- Pros and cons

...

A low test result in the stork test for a kayaker would not mean they are a poor performer given they don't require such good balance. Both sports require power to push through the gates and to jump up onto the board so the vertical jump test could provide a better indication of performance. However, the vertical jump test is based on power in the legs which aren't used so much in kayaking.

- Alternative arguments

...

In conclusion, both tests seem more relevant for surfers. They may provide some indication of performance, but there may be better ways to test the specific skills required in the performance of both disciplines.

- Conclusion is supported by evidence
- Justification linked to question

Which

Select one correct answer from a choice of four options provided.

Which of the following is not an effect of long-term strength and power training? [1]

- ☐ *Muscle hypertrophy*
- ☐ *Increased bone density*
- ☐ *Increased ligament strength*
- ☒ *Increased muscle length*

TOPICS FOR COMPONENT 3

Developing fitness to improve other participants performance in sport and physical activity

Information about the externally assessed exam:

Specification coverage

The importance of fitness for sports performance, fitness testing to determine fitness levels, and different fitness training methods.

The content for this assessment will be drawn from the essential subject content in Topics A to D of Component 3 in the specification.

Assessment

Written exam: 90 minutes

60 marks

All questions are mandatory

40% of the qualification grade

Assessment type: External synoptic

Guided learning hours: 48

Questions

A mix of short answer and longer answer questions assessing knowledge, understanding and skills in contextual scenarios building on all components within the qualification.

TYPES OF SPORTS REQUIRING SPECIFIC COMPONENTS OF FITNESS

Performance in sport can be improved by concentrating on the appropriate components of physical and skill-related fitness in training.

Team sports may require players to have different strengths depending on the position they play in. A rugby prop is likely to need greater power and strength, whereas a winger is likely to rely more on speed and agility.

Aerobic endurance – The ability of the heart and lungs to supply oxygen to the working muscles. Required for events and sports that last more than 30 minutes.

Marathon and endurance runners need to be able to maintain a high volume of oxygenated blood to the working muscles for a long period.

Muscular strength – The ability to overcome a resistance is useful for activities requiring force.

Javelin throwers require high muscular strength to force the javelin through the air over the furthest possible distance.

Speed – The ability to move body parts to perform an action quickly is useful for activities requiring fast movement.

Sprinters and **tennis players** require speed to move quickly across the track or court.

Muscular endurance – The ability of a muscle or muscle group to undergo repeated contractions, without fatigue. This is also required for events and sports that last more than 30 minutes.

Triathletes require muscular endurance for running, swimming and cycling to reduce fatigue in muscles repeatedly contracting.

Flexibility – The range of movement around a joint. Flexibility is useful for activities where performance is improved by greater movement.

Gymnasts, **divers**, **martial artists** and **figure skaters** require excellent flexibility to increase their range of movement and to reduce injury.

Body composition – The relative percentages of muscle and fat in the bodies of performers and athletes.

Rock climbers and **gymnasts** will favour a leaner body composition with a low percentage of fat. **Shot putters** and **sprinters** benefit from increased muscle mass.

Power can provide explosive movement required for high performance in some sporting disciplines.

Explosive strength (power), is crucial in **sprint sports**, **boxing**, **shot put** and **volleyball** to provide bursts of power when needed. For example, to get out of the blocks first, create a final burst to the finish line, put a shot or smash a ball with strength and speed.

Agility – The ability to move and change direction quickly (at speed) whilst maintaining control.

Rugby players need agility to dodge opposing defence players to avoid a tackle and gain territory.

Reaction time – The time taken to make a decision or initiate a response to a stimulus.

Sprint racers need to react to a starting gun quickly. **Boxers** need to avoid punches.

Balance – The control of the body's distribution of weight to remain upright and steady.

Windsurfers and **horse riders** need excellent balance to continually adjust their centre of mass to stay on top of their boards or horses as they move.

Coordination – The ability to use two or more body parts together smoothly and efficiently. This can also involve the use of equipment.

Ball and racket sports require excellent hand, eye and body coordination in order to strike the ball cleanly on a consistent basis.

Explain how the most important components of fitness for a football goalkeeper may differ from those of an outfield player. [4]

Goal keepers require good reaction times / power / coordination[1] *to save a penalty, jump or catch a ball.*[1] *Outfield players require high aerobic endurance / speed / agility*[1] *to run for 90 minutes, out pace their marker and dodge opponents.*[1]

THE BASIC PRINCIPLES OF TRAINING

The elements of FITT are useful in optimising a training plan in order to achieve fitness goals. FITT can also be used to apply the principle of progressive overload (page 5).

FITT

F Frequency

How often do training sessions happen? Frequency refers to the number of training sessions completed over a period of time, usually per week. Two or three times a week is considered a good start but this may increase as required.

I Intensity

How hard are the training sessions? Weights may be increased, resistance on a rowing machine may be increased or an incline may be introduced for runners.

T Time

How long do sessions last for? As fitness increases, sessions, reps or sets may increase. Rest periods may also decrease.

T Type

What type of training is done in each session? Type refers to how an individual will train by selecting a training method to improve a specific component of fitness **(see page 2)**. Switching between types of training **(pages 32–41)** adds variety, provides different fitness benefits and prevents boredom.

Which of the following methods could be used by a sprinter to increase the intensity of training? [1]

A Train at a lower altitude
B Increase rest periods
C Run uphill
D Attend more training sessions

C Run uphill.[1]

ADDITIONAL PRINCIPLES OF TRAINING

These additional principles of training are provided as guidance when designing a training programme. Following the principles of training will help to make training effective.

Progressive overload

Progress means to **gradually increase the intensity** of training so that fitness gains occur. Progress should be gradual in order to avoid injury. Overload is required to push your body beyond its comfortable limits to provide challenge, overcome plateaus in development and drive progress. Working harder than normal and putting your body under stress will result in adaptations and improvements to your body.

Specificity

Training programmes should be **specific to the sport**, in terms of training goals, movements, muscles used, intensity and energy systems. For example, to build specific muscle groups identified as needing improvement, or developing specific skills related to an athlete's sport, e.g. free or penalty kicks in field sports.

Individual differences

A **personal exercise plan** (**PEP**) should be created to suit the needs, age, gender and abilities of the individual so that it is of the right level of demand and considers any injuries.

Variation

Athletes should alter the type of training they use to avoid **boredom** and maintain **motivation**.

Rest and recovery

Sufficient time between training sessions should be given to allow the body to recover and adapt, and to allow participation in training to continue.

Adaptation

Over time, **changes to the body** will occur due to increased training loads. These may improve any of the components of fitness and as a result, the training programme may need to be adapted to maintain its impact and relevance.

Reversibility

Reversibility means that athletes will **undo their progress** if their training schedule lapses or becomes less demanding. Fitness gains from training and skill levels may decrease.

Time out through injury is the most common cause of reversibility.

Samira is training for a basketball match.

Explain how Samira can use the training principle of specificity to improve her performance in the game. [2]

Work on the muscles / movement / energy systems used in basketball.[1] *Work on agility with a ball to replicate the movements and intensity in a game.*[1] *Increase standing jump performance by working on the legs.*[1] *Practice set pieces or drills.*[1]

EXERCISE INTENSITY AND HOW IT CAN BE DETERMINED

Measuring intensity

Intensity of training or exercise can be measured by taking a heart rate reading. The higher the rate, the more intense the activity. The level of intensity has different demands on the body. Some fitness training methods (**page 32** to **41**) achieve better results at certain levels of intensity.

Calculating the aerobic and anaerobic training zone

The following formulae are used to calculate the correct training zone for a performer. For training to be most effective, the athlete must remain in the right target zone for their own fitness aims:

Maximum heart rate = 220 (Beats Per Minute) – Age

Aerobic training zone: 60% – 80% of maximum heart rate

Anaerobic training zone: 80% – 90% of maximum heart rate

Worked example

Abi is a 20 year old swimmer calculating her anaerobic training zone:

220 – 20 = 200 BPM Maximum heart rate

200 × 0.8 = 160 BPM Lower training threshold at 80% of MaxHR

200 × 0.9 = 180 BPM Upper training threshold at 90% of MaxHR

Abi should adapt her training so that her heart remains in the 160–180 BPM range in order to achieve maximum anaerobic benefit.

One Rep Max: Test for strength

The **one rep max** (**1RM**) test **(page 19)** commonly uses a bar bell, bench or leg press machine. It is used to determine the maximum weight that a particular muscle group can lift in one repetition (rep).

Choose an appropriate piece of weightlifting equipment for the muscle group being tested.

1. Lift an appropriate starting weight once. Use a spotter if necessary.
2. Increase the weight and lift again.
3. Repeat until the participant can no longer lift one rep.
4. Record the weight (usually in kg) of the last successful lift.

15 Rep Max: Test for muscular endurance

The **15 rep max test** seeks to determine the heaviest weight that can be lifted for 15 consecutive exercise repetitions.

The Borg (6–20) Rating of Perceived Exertion (RPE) Scale

The Borg scale is used by an individual to determine their own level of exertion based on how they feel. They can then increase or decrease their activity based on their own rating.

Rating	Likely BPM	Perceived exertion level	Description
6	60	Rest or very, very light activity	Sitting in a chair with little or no effort.
7	70		
8	80		
9	90	Very light	General day-to-day activity or a gentle walk.
10	100		
11	110	Fairly light	
12	120	Somewhat hard	Comfortable exercise with moderate effort. Able to hold a conversation.
13	130		
14	140		
15	150	Hard	Challenging activity that can only be maintained for 30–60 minutes.
16	160		
17	170	Very hard	The hardest exercise. Uncomfortable and difficult to speak. Laboured breathing.
18	180		
19	190	Very, very hard	
20	200	Maximal exertion	Absolute maximum.

Note the relationship between heart rate and RPE. Generally, RPE rating × 10 = HR (BPM)

Technology to measure exercise intensity

Heart rate monitors

A **heart rate monitor** is commonly worn on the wrist or around the chest. It can also be a sensory pad or handgrip on exercise equipment. It measures the changing heart rate and can sometimes provide a visual log of activity in graphical form.

Smart watches

A **smart watch** measures the changes in blood flow with each heartbeat to determine the beats per minute.

Apps

Some **apps** use the phone's camera to detect a pulse in the fingers when held over the lens. Others can be connected to a heart rate monitor or smartwatch which can then provide statistics, graphs, alerts and progress indicators for fitness programmes.

Henry is a 30 year old lacrosse player. He wants to increase his cardiovascular endurance in the aerobic zone. Describe how he could work out the upper and lower threshold of his aerobic training zone. [3]

220 – (age) 30 = 190 BPM Maximum heart rate[1] *× 60–80%*[1]

190 × 0.8 = 152[1] *BPM Upper training threshold at 80% of MaxHR*

190 × 0.6 = 114[1] *BPM Lower training threshold at 60% of MaxHR*

EXAMINATION PRACTICE

1. Darren plays tennis and begins training harder, and for longer.
   (a) Which training principle is Darren using? [1]
   - ☐ A – Specificity
   - ☐ B – Progressive overload
   - ☐ C – Reversibility
   - ☐ D – Rest and recovery

   (b) Which **one** of the following sports requires high agility? [1]
   - ☐ A – Freestyle skiing
   - ☐ B – Javelin
   - ☐ C – Sprinting
   - ☐ D – Weightlifting

   Agility, balance, fast reaction time, strength and coordination are all useful components of fitness for a tennis player.

   (c) State what is meant by agility. [1]

   (d) Name **one** other component of fitness useful to a tennis player.
   State why this is important for a tennis player. [2]

2. Jason plays football for his local team. He applies the basic principles of training, FITT.
   (a) Which **one** of the following represents the 'F' in FITT? [1]
   - ☐ A – Frequency
   - ☐ B – Friendship
   - ☐ C – Force
   - ☐ D – Future

   Jason is starting to find that his training is getting easier and becoming less effective.

   (b) Give **two** ways in which Jason can increase the intensity of his training. [2]

   Jason uses the Borg (6–20) Rating of Perceived Exertion (RPE) scale in his training.

   (c) Give **one** example of an activity likely to get a 6–8 on the scale. [1]

   (d) Jason perceived his activity level to be a 14.
   Give his likely peak heart rate during the activity. [1]

   Jason is 50 years old.

   (e) Calculate his maximum heart rate. [1]

   (f) Jason uses a heart rate monitor during exercise. It reads a peak at 145 BPM.
   State whether Jason is training in the aerobic or anaerobic zone at this heart rate.
   Show your working. [2]

   (g) Name **one** additional type of technology used to measure exercise intensity. [1]

(h) Jason also enjoys distance running and playing golf.
Identify the most relevant component of fitness for each of the two sports in pictures **A and B**.
Draw a straight line to match each picture to the most appropriate component of fitness. [2]

Picture A

Picture B

- Aerobic endurance
- Coordination
- Muscular strength
- Speed

3. Using the components of fitness, assess how a good gymnast may be able to transfer their skills to learn freestyle skiing. [6]

IMPORTANCE OF FITNESS TESTING

Fitness testing provides baseline data for monitoring or improving performance.

Reasons for fitness testing

- **Baseline data** can be used to design training programmes based on initial test results.
- After a period of training, the initial data can then be compared to determine if training programmes are working, and how well.
- Results can give a performer something to aim for.
- Results provide aims for use in goal setting. See **page 51** for SMARTER targets.

An explain question requires a point with a reason. Use connective words such 'because', 'in order to' or 'so that' to help gain that second mark.

A gymnastics centre regularly tests its members' fitness. Explain **one** reason why the testing equipment should be calibrated before each round of testing. [2]

To produce the same results / results to the same degree of accuracy each time the test is run.[1] *So that the results from one session can be fairly compared to those from another / so that results for different athletes can be more accurately compared with each other / with national benchmarks or testing scores.*[1]

Pre-test procedures

Calibration of equipment

Equipment must be **calibrated** to ensure that it provides **consistently accurate readings** and data.

To do this, readings are compared to known measurements of **time**, **weight** or **distance** for example. Adjustments are then made to the equipment as necessary until the readings match those expected.

Participant pre-fitness test check

This determines what prior exercise a participant has done, when, how regularly and at what intensity. It then takes into account their age and basic fitness levels before creating a personal exercise plan that is suitable for them and least likely to cause injury.

INFORMED CONSENT AND PAR-Q ASSESSMENTS

Informed consent ensures that a participant of physical activity is aware of what they are becoming involved in. **PAR-Q** stands for **Physical Activity Readiness Questionnaire**. A PAR-Q assessment is a short questionnaire to help trainers, coaches or fitness centre staff to determine any risks or safety considerations for an individual based on their health and medical history.

Informed consent

An **informed consent form** is signed by the participant prior to activity to confirm they understand the procedures in any training programme and associated risks. It may also outline the potential benefits and reasons for activity.

A signed informed consent form provides legal cover for a trainer or sports club should a participant injure themselves in their care.

PAR-Q

PAR-Q assessments are carried out before an individual begins any kind of fitness work in order:

- To review medical history
- To determine any potential heart conditions that may make training unsafe
- To assess readiness for safe exercise
- To make recommendations for amendments to a training or personal exercise programme (PEP) based on any health issues.

PARQ Health Questionnaire

Please read the questions carefully and answer honestly by ticking the appropriate box and/or adding information if necessary. Your response will be kept in strict confidence.

This form must be completed and returned to your Fitness Advisor and assessed prior to any induction.

Name:

Have you ever been diagnosed with a heart problem? Y N

In the past month have you had any chest pain when:

Doing an activity Y N You were resting Y N

Are you taking any medication for:

A heart condition Y N Any other problems Y N

Do you suffer from any bone and/or joint problems? Y N

In the past year have you had any major illnesses or surgery? Y N

Have you ever been diagnosed with:

Diabetes Y N Epilepsy Y N Other problems Y N

Asthma Y N

Are you pregnant? Y N Recently had a baby? Y N

If you've recently had a baby, how long ago was the birth?

Do you ever lose your balance or consciousness? Y N

Are you currently feeling unwell? (E.g. due to a cold.) Y N

If you have answered YES to one or more of the questions above, we may need to contact your doctor before starting an exercise plan.

If any of your responses change to a YES, please tell your Fitness Advisor as soon as possible.

I have read, understood and completed this questionnaire to the best of my knowledge. Any questions I had were answered satisfactorily by my Fitness Advisor.

Signed: Date:

1. Give **one** example of someone who may ask people for a PAR-Q assessment. [2]
2. Give **two** pieces of information that should be included in an informed consent form. [2]

1. Answers include: Teacher responsible for students using a weights room.[1] Fitness instructor working in a gym.[1] Personal trainer.[1] Performance coach.[1]

2. Personal details,[1] date,[1] signature,[1] training risks or testing details.[1]

REQUIREMENTS FOR THE ADMINISTRATION OF FITNESS TESTS

Test administrators need to know how to accurately set up and follow the rules of each fitness test. They will also need to record the data from fitness tests and compare the results to standardised data tables to interpret the results.

Knowledge of published standard test methods and equipment

Test administrators need to know how to implement each fitness test according to national or international standards and rules. Errors can occur in the results without the correct **knowledge of the test**, its **purpose** and its **rules**.

Accurate measurement and recording of test results

It is crucial that measurements are taken **accurately** and that test results are **correctly recorded**. A proper results data sheet should be used to record the results as they happen. Equipment appropriate for the test must also be checked, according to the rules and calibrated before the test. See **page 10**.

Basic processing of test results for interpretation

Once the test results have been accurately measured and recorded, some basic processing may be required for interpretation or they may be directly compared to published national or international standard data or scoring tables.

Selecting the appropriate test

Test administrators need to have a full knowledge of the purpose of each test, the situation in which they are using it and the needs of the participants in the test. This ensures that the right test is used for the right athletes, to test for the right skills or components of fitness.

For example, the hand grip dynamometer test measures muscular strength but only really the strength in the hand so this may be more suited to a rock climber than a sprinter.

Validity of results

Accuracy of measurement is crucial for tests to be meaningful and valid. For a test to be considered fair and valid, it also needs to measure a fair component of fitness that is relevant to the sport. For example, the vertical jump test measures power, but this is more valid for a basketball player than for a boxer.

Reliability of testing

Consistency of results is essential if test results are to be meaningful. The same test, applying the same set of rules correctly each time, should give the same results assuming the participant has no change in ability.

Factors affecting reliability

- **Calibration of equipment:** (See **page 10**.)
- **Motivation of the participant:** Motivation is difficult to make consistent, but it will impact results from one day to another. Participants (and their test administrators) may want to understand what drives them to perform well in a test. (See **page 50**.)
- **Conditions of the testing environment:** Tests should always be conducted in the same environment, indoors or outdoors. Weather, temperature and track surface conditions can affect results. For example, a strong head wind or cooler water temperature can slow down performance in the Cooper test. Temperature can also affect the performance of the working muscles.
- **Experience of the person administering the test:** More experienced testing administrators may be more confident and consistent with their application of the test. Compliance with standardised test procedures often gets better with experience, with less bending of the rules.

Practicality

Factors affecting practicality

- **Cost:** Tests that are expensive to administer cannot be run so often.
- **Time taken to perform the test:** Tests such as the 15RM test may take more time than is available, often more than a lesson in school.
- **Time taken to set up the test:** Some tests, such as the Illinois agility test, can take a long time to measure out and set up accurately and consistently with the rules.
- **Time taken to analyse data:** How easy is it to analyse the data or is it simply a comparison with a standard set of tables? The ruler drop test (**page 26**) can require some simple maths to determine the score. Other test results can be directly compared to normative tables.
- **Number of participants that can take part in the test at any time:** Some tests lend themselves well to a group to perform at the same time. Others are only designed for one person at a time, or require more equipment (such the grip dynamometer) that increases the cost for simultaneous group testing. This can also influence the practicality in terms of time.

Explain why it is important to calibrate the weighing scales for a boxer before a weigh-in. [2]

Boxers are governed by strict weight categories.[1] An inaccurate result on the scales could mean that a boxer is unfairly classed[1] and as such may cause an injury or an unfair bout result.[1]

FITNESS TEST METHODS FOR THE COMPONENTS OF PHYSICAL FITNESS

Each of the components of fitness can be linked to various sports and can help to plan, carry out, monitor and evaluate exercise and training programmes to suit individual needs.

Aerobic endurance

Aerobic endurance or **stamina** is the ability of the body to continue using energy from the aerobic energy system over a period of time. It can be measured using the multi-stage fitness test, the Yo-Yo test, the Harvard step test or the Cooper 12-minute run/walk test.

Marathon and endurance runners need aerobic endurance to be able to maintain a high volume of oxygenated blood to the working muscles for a prolonged period.

Multi-stage fitness (bleep) test

Cones, an assistant and a measuring tape of at least 20m in length are required to set up the **bleep test**. An audio player and recording of the bleeps is also required at the start.

When the assistant begins playing the recording of the bleeps, the participant must run 20 metres to reach the other cone before the next bleep. The time interval between bleeps gets progressively shorter, requiring faster and faster shuttle runs between the cones. Failure to reach the cone before the bleep, twice in a row, ends the test, and the last properly completed level should be recorded. The score is usually recorded as a level and bleep number, for example 5/7.

Cooper 12 minute run/swim test

Participants of the Cooper test aim to cover as much distance as they can in 12 minutes using a **track** (or pool), some **distance markers**, **recording sheets** and a **stopwatch**. Distance is usually measured in kilometres or miles. The test can be carried out on multiple people at the same time.

Expected performance is based on gender and age, but range between a score of 'Excellent' over 2800 metres for a male in his twenties, and a score of 'Poor' with 1100 metres for a woman in her fifties.

Kenneth Cooper MD created the Cooper test in 1968 to measure the maximum amount of oxygen that a person can use during exercise.

The test is still used in the military for stamina.

Aerobic endurance continued

Yo-Yo test

Like the bleep test, the **Yo-Yo test** involves running 20 metres between cones at increasing speeds governed by an audio track, but it offers a 10 second rest after each 40-metre shuttle. After each rest period, participants should come to a standing stop at the start cone again. The score is the overall distance covered or level reached in the last successful shuttle.

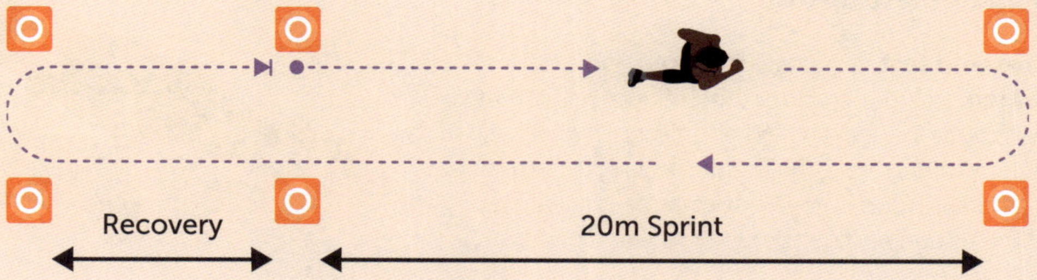

Harvard step test

A **bench** and a **timer** is required for this test.

Participants of the Harvard step test should step on and off a standard gym bench once every two seconds for five minutes. Their pulse should be measured one minute after finishing, and again at two and three minutes after finishing. The score is calculated as:

30,000 ÷ (Pulse 1 + Pulse 2 + Pulse 3).

1. The normative data for the Harvard step test (age 16) is provided below.

Gender	Excellent	Above average	Average	Below average	Poor
Male	> 90.0	80.0–90.0	65.0–79.9	55.0–64.9	< 55
Female	> 86.0	76.0–86.0	61.0–75.9	50.0–60.9	< 50

Jim scored 79.4 in his most recent step test. Ellie scored 76.2.

(a) Evaluate the performance of Jim and Ellie. [3]

(b) Ellie tested again each month for three months. Her scores were 78.1, 80.3 and most recently 81.8. Predict her next score if she continued to test again next month. [1]

(a) Jim is average.[1] *Ellie is above average.*[1] *Even though Jim's score was better, his comparative performance as a male was not as good as Ellie.*[1] *Ellie has better cardiovascular fitness than Jim.*[1]

(b) Anywhere in the range 83–85.[1]

Muscular endurance

Muscular endurance is the ability of a muscle or muscle group to undergo repeated contractions, without fatigue. It can be measured using the press-up test, the sit-up test or the timed plank test.

Swimmers, **rowers** and **rock climbers** require muscular endurance to maintain their performance for prolonged periods.

One-minute press-up test

The **press-up test** requires a **flat area** and a **stopwatch**. Using the correct technique, participants start with their arms extended and perform as many press-ups in a minute as they can. Resting is permitted only in the raised position. Performance is measured according to age and gender.

One-minute sit-up test

The **sit-up test** requires a partner to support the feet and ankles, and to press play on an audio recording of progressively faster bleeps. The participant sits up and back down again to the rhythm of the bleeps.

As a **maximal test**, the sit ups continue until the participant can no longer keep time with the bleeps. The score is equal to the number of sit ups performed.

2. Evaluate the use of the press up test for a sprint cyclist. [2]

2. The test measures the muscular endurance of the upper body and arms only.[1] *Sprint cyclists need muscular endurance*[1] *but they rely on their leg muscles which are not tested using this method.*[1]

Timed plank test

The **timed plank test** measures (and improves) core muscular endurance. The aim is to maintain a plank position on a flat surface for as long as possible. Start a stopwatch as soon as you start the plank and record your time as soon as the hips are lowered.

Flexibility

Flexibility is a measure of the range of movement possible at a joint. It can be measured using the 'sit and reach' test, the calf muscle flexibility test or the shoulder flexibility test.

Gymnasts, **divers**, **martial artists** and **figure skaters** require excellent flexibility to increase their range of movement and to reduce injury.

Sit and reach test

Using a **sit and reach box**, the athlete sits on the floor with their bare feet flat against the box and their legs straight. The athlete then reaches forwards as far as possible to move the slider. The slider records how far in centimetres they are from zero (their feet).

3. Give **two** reasons why a participant may not perform well on the sit and reach test. [2]

3. Two from: Tight hamstrings / short inelastic muscles / did not stretch or warm up,[1] *injured,*[1] *related muscle groups are rarely used,*[1] *short arms and long legs,*[1] *males are generally less flexible,*[1] *the test may be measured or performed incorrectly,*[1] *lack of motivation to try.*[1]

Calf muscle flexibility test

The **calf muscle flexibility** test measures changes over time in an individual's calf flexibility or length.

Standing a short distance from a wall with the front foot flat in front of the other, bend the front knee forwards until it touches the wall. Move slowly back and repeat until you can no longer touch the wall. Measure the final distance from the wall to your toes.

Note

There are no standard tables for comparing the results of the calf muscle and shoulder flexibility tests of different individuals since arm and leg length influences results.

Shoulder flexibility test

The **shoulder flexibility test** involves holding a pole or towel in front of the body with your hands firmly at each end. Lift the stick or towel over your head and down your back.

Repeat the test, moving your hands closer together each time until the movement is no longer possible. Score the minimum distance between your hands.

Speed

Speed is the ability to move body parts to perform an action quickly. It can be measured using the 30m sprint test, or the 30m flying sprint test.

Sprinters and **tennis players** require speed to move quickly across a track or court.

30m sprint test

The **30m sprint test** measures acceleration and speed. It requires setting up two cones 30 metres apart using a measuring tape. After a proper warm up, the participant is timed using a stopwatch from the moment they leave the blocks or from a standing start.

30m flying sprint test

The **30 metre flying sprint test** measures speed between two points, but with a flying (moving) start. The participant is timed at full pace throughout the distance instead of using a standing start with the standard 30m test.

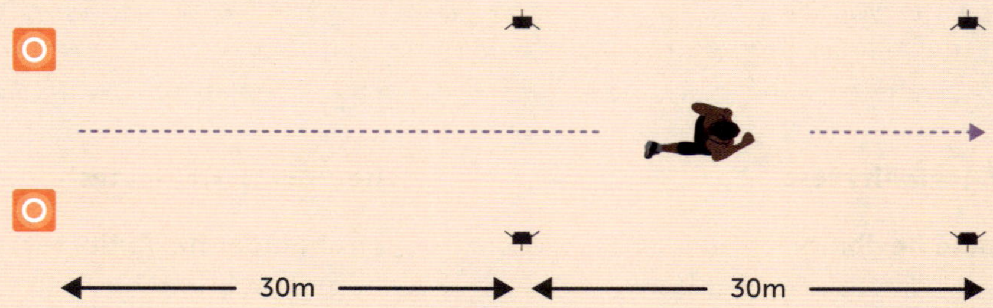

4. James is preparing to test himself and some teammates using the 30m flying sprint test.
   (a) The 30 metre flying sprint test measures speed. Describe how to carry out this test. [3]
   (b) James completes the test with his teammates. The table below shows their results.

Teammate	30 metre flying sprint test result (seconds)
James	3.5
Victoria	4.7
Troy	3.1
Ismail	4.4

   (i) State which teammate had the fastest performance. [1]
   (ii) Calculate the difference in time between the fastest and slowest participant. [1]

4. (a) Use 2 cones [1] and place them 30 metres apart using a tape measure. [1] Allow a 30m flying start to the sprint [1] and with a stop watch, time the athlete running as they pass between the start and end cones. [1] Record the time in seconds. [1]
(b) (i) Troy. [1] (ii) 4.7 – 3.1 = 1.6 seconds difference. [1]

Muscular strength

Muscular Strength is the maximum force a muscle, or group of muscles can apply against a resistance. It can be further categorised as maximal, static, dynamic and explosive strength. Strength can be measured using the grip strength dynamometer test or the 1 Repetition Maximum (RM) test.

High maximal strength is required in **boxing** and **weightlifting**. Static strength helps **rugby players** to hold the resistance in a scrum position. **Gymnasts** need high dynamic strength.

Grip strength dynamometer test

This measures **grip strength**. Using a handgrip dynamometer in the dominant hand, squeeze the handle with maximum effort keeping the elbow at 90 degrees. Record the best score.

1 repetition maximum (1RM) test

The **1 rep max test** measures the maximal weight that can be lifted in a single attempt. Using free weights or a specialised machine, and a spotter, a participant should select a suitable weight and lift it once using the correct technique. After a few minutes rest, they should increase the weight and try again, repeating this until they reach their maximum.

The 1RM test could be used to measure the strength of various muscle groups such as the quadriceps, latissimus dorsi, pectorals or biceps using different lifting techniques.

Body composition

Body composition refers to the percentages of fat, muscle and bone in the human body.

Rock climbers will favour a leaner body composition with a low percentage of fat. **Shot putters** benefit from increased body mass.

BMI (Body Mass Index)

The BMI table provides a rough approximation of obesity. Use the chart on the **right** to calculate your BMI.

5. State the BMI rating for an athlete weighing 90kg with a height of 180cm. [1]

'Overweight'. [1]

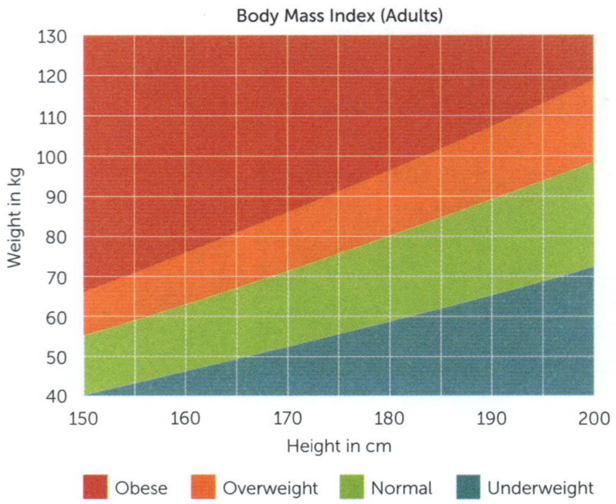

Bioelectrical Impedance Analysis (BIA)

Bioelectrical impedance devices are often integrated into bathroom weighing scales. The are used to calculate the electrical resistance of a low electrical signal passed through the body as you stand on the scales. Since bone and fat cause greater resistance than muscle, it can approximate the composition of the body based on pre-given variables such as height, weight, gender, level of fitness and age.

Water conducts electricity well, so a well hydrated performer can show an underestimate of fat.

Waist to hip ratio

The **waist to hip ratio** is calculated as a measurement of the waist circumference divided by the hip circumference. This is a simple home test using a tape measure to determine the likely level of belly fat. A lower ratio is shown to reduce the risk of heart disease and diabetes.

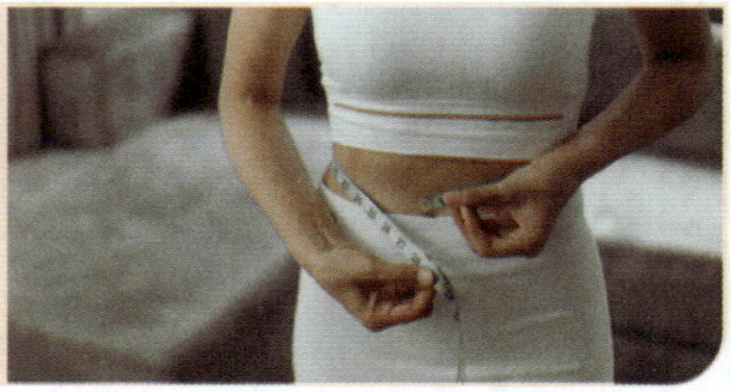

FITNESS TEST METHODS FOR THE COMPONENTS OF SKILL-RELATED FITNESS

Each of the components of fitness can be linked to various sports and can help to plan, carry out, monitor and evaluate exercise and training programmes to suit individual needs.

Agility

Agility is the ability to move and change the direction of your body quickly whilst maintaining control.

Rugby players need agility to sidestep around opposing players to avoid a tackle and gain territory.

Illinois agility run test

This test measures agility. It requires **eight cones**, carefully arranged at measured distances apart as shown in the diagram.

The performer starts face down and runs against a **stopwatch timer** to the end. The activity is measured in seconds.

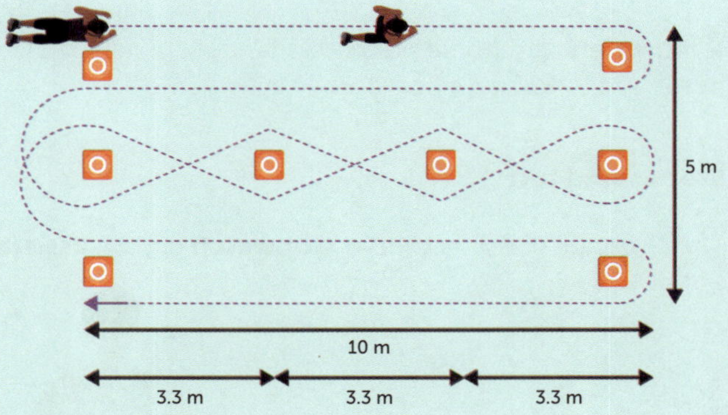

T test

The **T test** measures agility of movement forwards as well as sideways and backwards which can be a more valid way of testing for specific sports that may commonly involve backwards and lateral running such as **tennis**.

The T test involves running forwards from cone A to cone B. Then sidestep left to touch cone C, sidestep right to touch cone D and back to B. Then backwards to return to cone A. A timer is started and stopped as the performer leaves and returns to cone A.

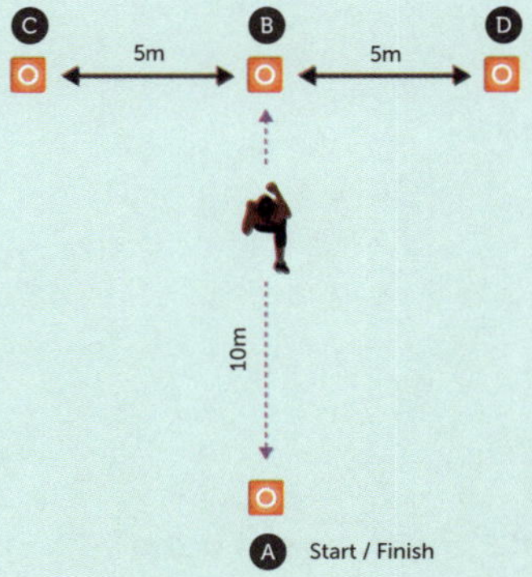

1. Speed and agility are useful in sports that require sudden changes of direction, such as football and badminton. The table below shows some test results for a group of male <18 football players.

Performer	30 metre (seconds	Illinois agility test (seconds)
Joe	4.2	15.8
Karl	4.6	16.4
Mason	4.3	16.3

(a) Which player appears to be slowest? [1]
(b) Which player has the greatest agility? [1]

(a) Karl[1] *(b) Joe*[1]

Balance

Balance is defined as the ability to stay upright or stay in control of body movement. The body's centre of mass is kept above its base. Balance can be measured using the 'stork stand' test or the Y balance test.

Windsurfers and **horse riders** need excellent balance to continually adjust their centre of mass to stay on top of their boards or horses as they move.

Stork stand test

The stork stand test requires a **stopwatch** and an **assistant**. Time is recorded in seconds.

1. Start from a balanced position on two feet.
2. Place hands on hips.
3. Place one foot on the inside of the knee of the standing leg.
4. Lift the heel of the standing leg when stopwatch is started.
5. Stop the timer when balance is lost or when the foot moves from the inside leg.

Test yourself using the standard national ratings given here.

Rating	Males (seconds)	Females (seconds)
Excellent	> 50	> 30
Good	41–50	23–30
Average	31–40	16–22
Fair	20–30	10–15
Poor	< 20	< 10

Balance continued

Y balance test

The Y balance test requires a **2 x 2 metre space**, a **Y balance test kit** or some **sticky tape** and a **measuring tape**. Performance should be recorded on a record sheet.

This test measures **core control** as well as **dynamic balance** which may be more suitable for testing gymnasts than the stork stand test.

A B C

Starting with the right foot in the centre and the hands on the hips, the participant should reach their left foot as far as possible in front of them in three attempts and mark the furthest distance, shown in figure A. They should then repeat this with the other foot. The process can then be repeated again for the posterior positions in figures B and C. The participant cannot touch their foot down on the floor to regain balance during an attempt.

2. Evaluate the appropriateness of the Stork Stand Test for a gymnast and a cyclist. [6]

The stork stand test is a maximal test. It measures static balance.[✓] *The test can easily be carried out by a cyclist or gymnast as it requires no equipment / can be completed anywhere.*[✓] *Static strength may be used by a cyclist in a starting position or by a gymnast holding a pose.*[✓] *A gymnast needs excellent static balance which this measures.*[✓] *Gymnasts often need to balance on one leg which is also measured in this test.*[✓] *A cyclist requires good balance on their bike but not on their own feet*[✓] *and would not replicate the movements of their sport so closely*[✓] *so the test results may not be such a reliable measure of performance.*[✓] *The test could be useful to measure improvement in balance for both athletes.*[✓] *Overall, the test would be better for identifying strengths and weaknesses in a gymnast's balance than a cyclist's.*[✓]

This question should be marked in accordance with the levels-based mark scheme on page 59.

Coordination

Coordination is the ability to move two or more body parts under control, smoothly and efficiently. It can be measured using the 'wall toss' test or the stick flip coordination test.

Ball and racket sports require excellent hand, eye and body coordination in order to strike the ball cleanly on a consistent basis.

Alternate-hand wall-toss test

The **wall toss test** measures **hand-eye coordination**. It requires a **tennis ball**, a **flat wall**, some **marker tape** or **chalk**, and a **stopwatch**.

1. Mark a point or line 2 metres away from a flat wall.
2. Stand at the line with both feet together facing the wall.
3. Start the stopwatch or timer for 30 seconds.
4. Throw the ball at the wall with one hand and catch it in the other.
5. Repeat this, throwing from one hand to the other as many times as possible in the time.
6. Record the score counting each successful catch as 1.

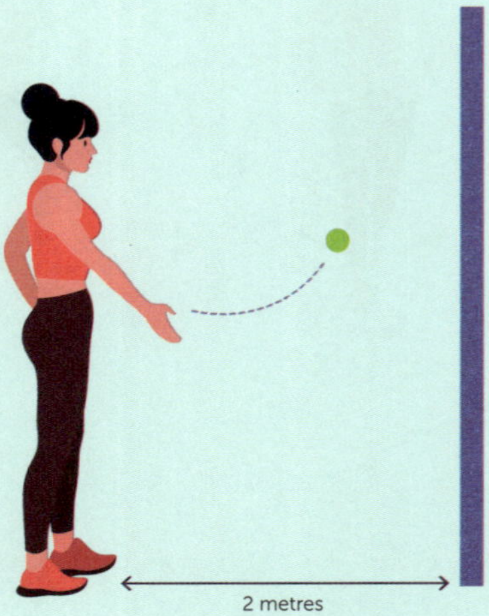

Stick flip coordination test

A cut down wooden broom handle can make an excellent set of sticks for this test using the rounded top acting as the marker end.

The **stick flip test** requires **three sticks**, each about 60cm long and 25mm in diameter, with some tape or a marker at the end of one of them.

The performer has three practice attempts, then five attempts to perform a half flip of the centre baton (so that the marker faces in the opposite direction). If it lands successfully balanced on the other two sticks held in each hand, it counts as a successful half flip and scores one point. Five attempts at the full flip are then allowed, being awarded two points for each successful attempt. A maximum of 15 points is awarded.

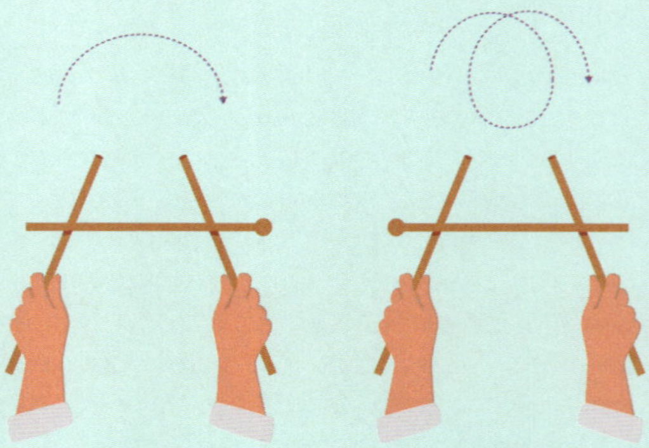

Power

Power (or **explosive strength**) is the product of strength and speed, i.e. strength × speed. Power can be measured using the vertical jump test, the standing long/broad jump test or the Margaria-Kalamen power test.

Quick bursts of power are important when performing in **sprint sports**, **boxing**, **shot put** and **volleyball**. For example, to get out of the blocks first, to create a final burst to the finish line, put a shot or to smash a ball with strength and speed.

Vertical jump test

The **vertical jump test** involves a **wall**, a **ruler** or **measuring tape**, and some **chalk** to make a mark with. With flat feet, stand and reach up the wall as high as possible and record the height.

Now, jump as high as possible using your arms and legs and make a mark using chalked hands or ask an assistant to record the height. Measure the distance between the standing reach height and the jump height in centimetres.

Standing long/broad jump test

The **standing long jump test** also measures leg power. Participants stand with their feet slightly apart behind a marked line. Swinging the arms for momentum, they jump (and land) two-footed as far as possible. A measurement is taken from the take off line to the back of the landing heel.

Margaria-Kalamen power test

The **Margaria-Kalamen power stair test** measures the power in the lower body to climb stairs. Using a run up of six metres in front of some 'standard' steps. Markers are placed on step 3 and step 9. A stopwatch is started when the foot hits step 3 and stopped on step 9.

The **score** is calculated using a formula where mass is the weight in kg of the participant and distance is the vertical difference in height between steps 3 and 9. 9.8 is the constant of gravity:

$$\text{Power} = (\text{Mass} \times \text{Distance}) \times 9.8 / \text{time}$$

For the test to be reliable, you need stairs of the correct height and steepness, with a clear run up area. It is also more difficult to time unless using timing mats.

Reaction time

Reaction time is the ability to respond quickly to a stimulus. It can be measured using the ruler test or an online reaction time test.

Sprint racers need to react to a starting gun quickly. **Boxers** need to avoid punches.

Ruler drop test

Reaction times become slower as people age.

Requirements: A **metre rule** and an **assistant**.

1. The assistant holds the metre rule vertically at the zero end.
2. The participant places their thumb and forefingers around the stick or rule at the 50cm mark but without touching it.
3. The stick is released by the assistant without warning.
4. The participant must close their fingers around the stick as fast as possible to catch it.
5. The score is the distance in centimetres from the catching point to the original 50cm mark.

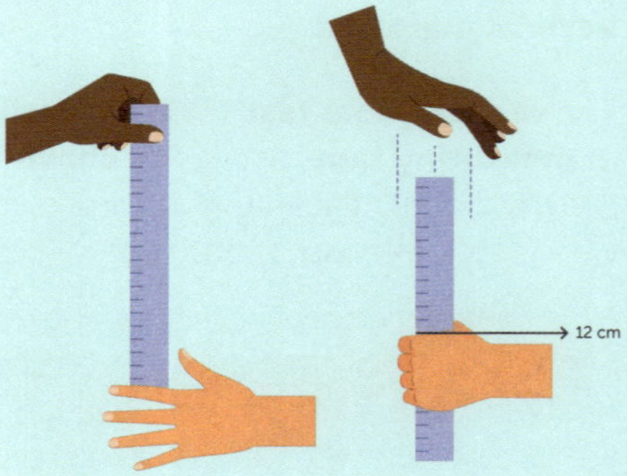

Online reaction time test

Various online reaction time tests exist. They generally require you to click a button to start the test and again when you see a change in colour of another object, screen background or traffic light. An average of five attempts is commonly calculated and provided.

3. Figure 1 shows the ruler test reaction scores for three athletes in training over a 10 week period. Using the information in Figure 1, describe the three athletes' performance and progress. [3]

Figure 1

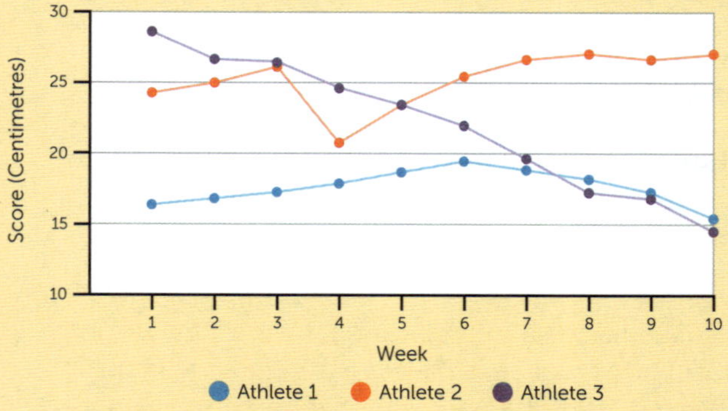

Athlete 1 had the fastest reaction time but got worse over the first five tests until they started to improve again after six weeks.[1] *Athlete 2 showed relatively little change over the period but had a significant improvement in the middle.*[1] *Athlete 3 started relatively poorly but made the most progress with the fastest score of the three by week 10.*[1]

INTERPRETATION OF FITNESS TEST RESULTS

Most fitness tests have a set of published, normative (standard) data with which your own test results can be compared to get a better sense of performance.

Comparing results to normative published data

Once an initial test has been completed, the results can be compared to national or international standard data. After the first test, test results can be compared to historic test results to provide an indication of progress over time.

Results may also be compared to other performers, but height, weight and gender can make this less valid.

1. The table below shows the standard ratings for the wall-toss test.

Rating	Excellent	Good	Average	Fair	Poor
Score (in 30 seconds)	> 35	30–35	20–29	15–19	< 15

Joel scored 22. What was his rating? [2]

Average.[1]

Making recommendations for improvements based on test results

The following is an example set of normative data commonly used to assess the performance of women in the press up test.

Age	Excellent	Good	Average	Fair	Poor
20–29	> 48	34–38	17–33	6–16	< 6
30–39	> 39	25–39	12–24	4–11	< 4
40–49	> 34	20–34	8–19	3–7	< 3
50–59	> 29	15–29	6–14	2–5	< 2
60+	> 19	5–19	3–4	1–2	< 1

You may be asked to analyse and evaluate test results. The questions on this page and **pages 14–26** provide examples of this sort of question.

2. Sally is 32 years old. She has completed her first press up test with a score of 10.

Assess how Sally could improve her fitness based on her results in the press up test. [6]

The press up test assesses core strength and muscular strength in the arms.[1] *Sally's initial score was 'fair'.*[1] *She could concentrate on increasing her repetitions using weights in the gym*[1] *and increase the weight she can lift using either the 1RM or 15RM methods.*[1] *This would increase her arm strength*[1] *and could increase the number of press ups she is able to do.*[1] *Sally could also lower her BMI*[1] *if that is high as she may be lifting unnecessary bodyweight.*[1] *She could eat more healthily to lose excess body fat.*[1] *This could be assessed using the waist to hip ratio.*[1] *The timed plank test could also be used to develop core strength.*[1]

This question should be marked in accordance with the levels-based mark scheme on page 59.

EXAMINATION PRACTICE

Topic B: Investigate fitness testing to determine fitness levels

1. Andrea plays hockey for her local club. She has undertaken her first physical fitness yo-yo test to provide some baseline data.
   (a) Explain the need for baseline data. [2]
   (b) Give **one** other reason for fitness testing. [1]

   Andrea is told by her coach that she can participate in a skill-related fitness test in the following week of training.

   (c) Complete Table 1 by:
      (i) Naming **two** types of skill-related fitness tests. [2]
      (ii) Identify the related component of fitness that each test measures. [2]

(i) Type of skill-related fitness test	(ii) Related component of fitness
[1]	[1]
[1]	[1]

Table 1

   Andrea completes a PAR-Q questionnaire and signs a form before participating in the yo-yo test to confirm she understands the risks involved.

   (d) Give the name of this form. [1]
   (e) Which **one** of the following is not found on a PAR-Q questionnaire? [1]
      ☐ A – Current state of health
      ☐ B – Declaration of existing heart conditions
      ☐ C – Dietary information
      ☐ D – Medical history
   (f) Give **one** reason why a personal trainer would ask a client to complete a PAR-Q assessment before activity commences. [1]
   (g) Assess how Andrea could ensure the yo-yo test results are valid before the test begins. [6]

2. Kyle is involved in a variety of sporting activities during a summer school programme. He considers himself to have good reaction time, aerobic endurance and power.

(a) In which of these sporting activities is reaction time most important? [1]

- ☐ A – Lawn bowls
- ☐ B – Motor racing
- ☐ C – Snooker
- ☐ D – Target shooting

(b) Which pair of fitness tests assess aerobic endurance? [1]

- ☐ A – 30m sprint test and the yo-yo test
- ☐ B – Cooper 12-minute run/swim test and the 30m sprint test
- ☐ C – Cooper 12-minute run/swim test and the Harvard step test
- ☐ D – Sit and reach test and the Harvard step test

(c) Kyle enjoys playing rugby for his school and an outside club.

Some player positions in rugby require more power than others.

(i) What is meant by 'power'? [1]

(ii) Suggest **one** other sporting activity where power would be an advantage. [1]

(iii) Give **one** suitable test for power. [1]

(d) Kyle and Michelle have been taking the Illinois agility run test as part of their club training.

They are both 16 years old. Kyle's time was 17.1 seconds. Michelle's time was 17.2 seconds.

Analyse the data in **Table 2**.

Describe what it shows about Kyle and Michelle's performance and level of agility. [3]

Performance category	Males aged 16–19 (sec)	Females aged 16–19 (sec)
Excellent	< 15.2	< 17.0
Good	15.2–16.1	17.0–17.9
Average	16.2–18.1	18.0–21.7
Fair	18.2–18.3	21.8–23.0
Poor	> 18.3	> 23.0

Table 2: National standards for the Illinois agility test

3. An outdoor activity centre offers rock climbing and kayaking. They have competitive teams for both sports that compete against people from other centres.

The centre trainer has decided to use a handgrip dynamometer test to measure the strength of competitors in both sports.

(a) Describe how to carry out this test. [3]

(b) Evaluate whether the test is more relevant to a rock climber or a kayaker. [6]

WARM-UPS

Warm-ups gradually increase the oxygen going to the working muscles, increasing temperature and flexibility. Warm-ups also raise the heart rate in preparation for exercise.

Benefits of warming up

Warming up should include an activity that **gradually raises the pulse**, ready for exercise. **Stretching the muscles increases pliability, mobility and flexibility**, and **reduces the risk of injury**. Sports related skills and drills are also commonly included. This increases the amount of oxygen to the working muscles and provides **mental preparation** so that the athlete is ready for the main training session or competition.

1 Pulse raising

- Warms up muscles and prepares the body for physical activity.
- Raises body temperature slowly.
- Gradually raises heart rate up to full pace to avoid physical or mental shock.

2 Mobility and stretch

Mobility takes joints through their full range of movement in order to loosen them, for example shoulder rotations, lunges and lateral rotations of the neck.

- The range of movement is increased.
- Improves the flexibility of muscles and joints.

3 Reduce the risk of injury

- Warm muscles are less likely to tear.
- Increased mobility reduces the risk of injury.

4 Prepare the body for exercise

Core or common skills used in a game may be part of a warm up practice, for example, a tennis player may practice serves, volleys, back hands and forehand shots.

- Psychological preparation and confidence.
- The practice of skills through the whole range of movement.

Explain why it is important to warm up before an intensive training session. [3]

Three from: Gradually increase heart rate in preparation for exercise.[1] *Gradually increase blood flow around the body to warm muscles.*[1] *Stretch and lengthen muscles to increase range of motion to prevent injury before stress.*[1] *Increase oxygen flow to the working muscles in preparation for exercise.*[1] *Prepare the mind for intense exercise and focus on training.*[1] *Encourage blood flow to divert from the inactive organs to the active muscles.*[1]

COOL DOWNS

Cool down activities after a period of exercise should include moderate, but not intense exercise, similar to those used for warm-ups. Cooling down enables an athlete to train more frequently, to avoid injury and to achieve better results.

Benefits of cooling down

Cooling down requires maintaining an elevated breathing and heart rate by including a walk or jog, for example. Stretching allows muscles to lengthen whilst warm and then relax. A gradual reduction in intensity prevents overheating, light-headedness and nausea.

It also provides an opportunity to increase post exercise oxygen consumption and encourages blood to redistribute around the body.

Benefits of cooling down include:

- **Gradually lower pulse** and breathing rate to resting levels which reduces the risk of blood pooling and dizziness.
- The removal of **lactic acid**, CO_2 and waste products from the working muscles.
- **Stretching** helps return muscles to pre-exercise length, and develops flexibility.
- To reduce (delayed onset) muscle soreness (DOMS).

Ronny plays football for his local team.

Give **one** way that Ronny could cool down after a match. [1]

Stretching exercises,[1] gentle jog / low intensity movements.[1]

FITNESS TRAINING METHODS FOR THE PHYSICAL COMPONENTS OF FITNESS

Each of the training methods on the next pages relate to an associated component of fitness. For each training method, the basic principles of training (FITT) and the additional principles of training should be applied.

Aerobic endurance

Continuous training

Continuous training involves sustained exercise at a **constant rate** (or **steady state**) with **no rest**. It involves **aerobic demand** for a minimum of 30 minutes, for example running, swimming, rowing or cycling.

Advantages
Many athletes can take part at the same time.
Easy to set up with minimal equipment required. Can usually be done without access to specialist facilities, e.g. a park.
Very effective at improving aerobic (cardiovascular) and muscular endurance for long distance athletes.
Closely replicates the demands of distance or endurance sports.

Disadvantages
Longer training sessions can take a lot of time out of the day.
Can result in tedium or boredom.
May need access to swimming pools, velodromes or running track.
Continuous movements may result in injury from repetitive contractions.

1. George is training for a marathon. He has chosen to use continuous training.
   Evaluate whether continuous training is an effective training method for George. [6]

Continuous training is sustained for at least 30 minutes at a constant pace.[✓] It is a form of training that has a relatively low impact on his joints and ligaments.[✓] This can help George to avoid injury.[✓] Continuous training by running can closely replicate the movements of a marathon[✓] and requires no specialist equipment.[✓] He is likely to improve his cardiovascular / aerobic endurance and may improve his body shape,[✓] reducing his weight[✓] and increasing speed.[✓] Continuous training is suitable for individuals as programmes need to be tailored which may suit George[✓] as he needs to follow a training programme that is suitable for his own level of fitness, challenge and experience.[✓] George may become bored[✓] by running constantly so could vary exercise with cycling or swimming.[✓] However, this would not replicate the movements of a marathon so closely.[✓] George could supplement his training[✓] with other techniques such as interval training and static stretching to increase strength and lengthen his stride / range of motion which would improve his performance.[✓]

This question should be marked in accordance with the levels-based mark scheme on page 59.

Aerobic endurance continued

Fartlek training

Fartlek is the Swedish term for 'speed play'. This involves **varying the speed**, **terrain** and **work:recovery ratios** of exercises. It is related to continuous training and interval training. Intensity is varied over different terrain, gradients or speed of activity.

Advantages	Disadvantages
No specialist equipment required.	Requires discipline to continuously undertake unstructured exercise.
Simple setup but route requires some thought to make it most suitable for the participant(s).	Programmes need to be tailored to the individual so only suitable for individuals or small groups with very similar requirements.
Commonly used by sports teams to improve speed, aerobic and muscular endurance.	Access to space with varied terrain required.
Replicates the stop/start nature of field sports.	Experience is required to ensure training is at the right intensity.

To improve aerobic endurance, performers should decrease the number or length of rest periods and decrease work intensity (compared to speed training). For improvement in speed, see high intensity interval training (HIIT) on page 38)

Interval training

Interval training involves periods of exercise, interspersed with periods of rest or low intensity exercise, for example five 100m sprints with a 200m jog in between.

Advantages	Disadvantages
No essential equipment required. May use a heart monitor or the RPE scale.	Can be hard to keep going which requires motivation.
Simple to arrange for all levels of experience.	Can be suitable for individuals or small groups of all ability levels.
Develops aerobic and anaerobic fitness depending on the intensity.	Access to indoor or outdoor space required.
Easily adapted for a range of sporting activities, specific outcomes and fitness components.	Intensity can cause injury if not performed within the aerobic or anaerobic thresholds.

Circuit training

Circuit training involves roughly 6–12 **stations**, each with a different exercise designed to achieve the aims of the participants. Station activities will depend on the **space** and **equipment** available. The demand of a circuit can be altered according to the exercise or by changing the **work:rest ratio** to decrease rest and achieve overload more quickly.

Circuit training can also be used to improve **muscular endurance** by using body resistance exercises or weights with low loads and high repetitions. See page 37.

Advantages
Usually involves little equipment so it is inexpensive to organise.
Easy to set up stations.
Effective at training the whole body or specific parts. Different exercises can replicate specific sporting movements.
Content or intensity can be specifically adapted to suit most training goals and to target most components of fitness.
A circuit can be set up almost anywhere.
Can be used by large groups, sometimes two to each station. (One rests while the other exercises.)

Disadvantages
Does not replicate 'real time' match play situations or competition.
Isolated exercises may not always be sport specific.
Technique can be affected by muscle fatigue which can increase the risk of injury.

2. The type of training should be adapted to ensure that the heart and body are working at the right level to achieve the fitness aims of the individual.

   Other than rest, give **one** way in which circuit training can be altered to determine the fitness aim. [2]

   Two from: Time,[1] content.[1]

Flexibility

Static active

Static active stretches are done alone. The performer applies and controls the amount of force to the stretch without assistance from another person.

Static passive

Static passive stretches involve the help of another person or an object, e.g. a wall, to apply an external force causing the muscle to stretch.

Advantages	Disadvantages
Active stretches can involve groups or individuals as stretches are all done independently with no specialist help, location or equipment required. Passive stretches may require the help of trainers.	Can take time to complete a full stretch of each muscle in the whole body. Boring.
Very effective at improving flexibility and range of motion at joints which aids performance and reduces sports injury.	Some muscle groups are difficult to stretch.
Not sport specific, but may replicate the demands of some sports, for example gymnastics.	Poor technique, bouncing a stretch or over stretching can cause injury.

3. Describe how stretching would be beneficial to the performance of **two** different sporting skills. [2]

Two from: Improved range of motion allows a diver to maintain a neat tuck or pike position,[1] *a hurdler can more easily raise the trailing leg over the hurdle,*[1] *a gymnast / figure skater benefits from greater flexibility.*[1]
Answers are not exhaustive.

Flexibility continued

Proprioceptive Neuromuscular Facilitation (PNF) technique

This technique is another form of passive stretching as it also commonly involves the use of a partner or immovable object.

1. Firstly, hold a muscle or muscle group in the stretch position.
2. Then contract this muscle against resistance while it's kept in the stretched position. This creates an isometric muscle contraction.
3. Stretch the muscle again to finish off.

Advantages
No specialist equipment required.
Highly effective in increasing flexibility and range of movement with quick results.
Boosts muscle strength.
Not sport specific, but may replicate the actions of some sports, for example wrestling or martial arts.

Disadvantages
Can take time to stretch the whole body.
Can require a trainer or physiotherapist which limits the number of participants.
Can reduce power if done before exercise, e.g. in sprinting.
Good communication between the participant and stretching partner is necessary to ensure a safe stretch.

An **isometric muscle contraction** occurs to hold a static position and does not create movement. The muscles will not change length as the muscle force is equal to the resistance.

4. Give **one** advantage of the Proprioceptive Neuromuscular Facilitation (PNF) stretching technique. [1]

One from: Increased range of motion [1]*, increased muscular strength* [1]*, increased muscle flexibility.* [1]

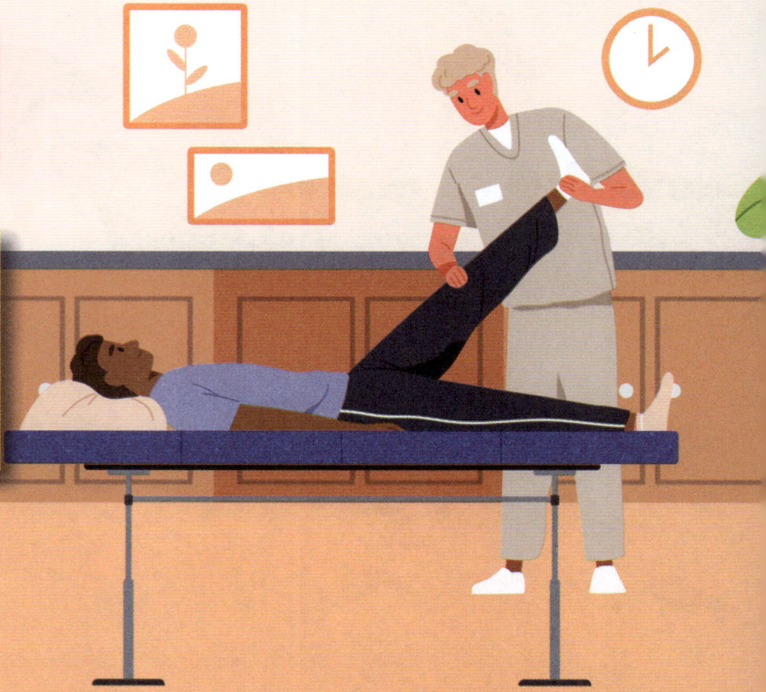

Muscular endurance

Free weights and fixed resistance machines

High repetitions and low loads allow performers to develop muscular endurance. Muscles are not overloaded but are encouraged to work repeatedly.

Circuit training

Circuit training can also be used to develop aerobic endurance by doing body resistance exercises or weights with low loads and high repetitions. See **page 34**.

Advantages	Disadvantages
Can have individual or group participation, sometimes two to a station. (One rests while the other exercises.)	May need access to a weightlifting gym or equipment. Equipment costs can vary.
Easy to set up circuit training stations. Machines take little training to use.	Lifting technique must be correct and can be affected by muscle fatigue which can increase the risk of injury.
Effective at training the whole body or specific parts. Different exercises can replicate specific sporting movements.	Does not replicate 'real time' match play situations or competition.

Muscular strength training

Free weights and fixed resistance machines

Standard gym weightlifting equipment and specialist resistance machines can be used to develop power in isolated muscle groups, e.g. triceps or pectorals) through **low repetitions and high loads**.

Advantages	Disadvantages
Can have individual or group participation, sometimes two to a station. (One spots or rests while the other exercises.)	Usually need access to a weightlifting gym or equipment. Equipment costs or gym fees can be high.
Free weights or resistance machines take little training to set up and use.	Lifting technique must be correct and can be affected by muscle fatigue which can increase the risk of injury.
Effective at improving muscular strength of targeted areas. Different exercises can replicate specific sporting movements, e.g. throwing.	Muscle ache a day or so after training is common.

Speed

Acceleration sprints

In acceleration sprint training, pace is gradually increased from a standing or rolling start to jogging, then to striding, and then to a maximal sprint. This helps to maintain the technical elements of sprinting whilst reducing the chances of injury. With each phase requiring about 50m of space, a long track is required.

Advantages
Can involve larger groups of people.
No specialist equipment required, and no cost to training. Easy to set up.
Effective at increasing speed and replicates the nature of match play in sport.

Disadvantages
Requires access to a large space to be able to sprint.
Can become repetitive and boring.
Gradual intensity reduces the risk of injury but a warm up is still required to avoid pulled muscles or strains.

Interval training

Interval training can be used for aerobic endurance and speed training depending on the intensity of the workouts and the periods of rest or active rest. For speed training, **high intensity interval training** is required using short, high intensity work periods, increasing the number of rest periods and increasing work intensity. See interval training for endurance on **page 33**.

Resistance drills

Resistance makes exercise more difficult which develops muscles through hypertrophy. When the resistance is removed, the muscles can work faster instead of harder. Resistance can be achieved through:

- **Hill runs** (or using an incline setting on an exercise machine)
- **Parachutes** (running with a chute behind you)
- **Sleds**, containing a weighted mass, or dragging an old tyre
- **Bungee ropes**
- **Resistance bands**

Advantages
Can be done with individuals or small groups if there is sufficient equipment.
Simple to set up once the equipment is available.
Effective at increasing speed, acceleration and functional strength which is an advantage for track events and field games such as rugby.
Low risk of injury.

Disadvantages
Need equipment (or a suitable hill) to provide the resistance. Parachutes can be difficult to inflate fully.
Cost of equipment can vary. Hills are free.

FITNESS TRAINING METHODS FOR SKILL-RELATED COMPONENTS OF FITNESS

There are many different types of skills-related training, each with their own distinctions.

Agility

Speed, agility and quickness training (SAQ)

SAQ involves drills to develop physical ability and motor skills. This develops **speed** and **agility** in combination, producing more explosive multi-directional movements. It also works on reaction time. Like high intensity interval training, SAQ predominately involves short bursts of anaerobic activity, but it concentrates on activities that are specifically suitable for speed and agility training, and the demands of your sport. This is the principle of **specificity**. See **page 5**.

Advantages
Suitable for individuals or small groups of people with similar requirements.
Specifically designed to replicate the demands of the sport.

Disadvantages
Comprises drills from various other elements of training where some will involve more equipment and complexity than others to set up, perform or measure.
Easy to overtrain or get injured if not properly managed.

1. Tom and Sally are preparing for an annual badminton tournament.
   Explain why SAQ training might be appropriate for them. [2]

1. SAQ training increases speed which is a specific component of fitness desirable to move across the court in badminton.[1] Agility is required to change direction quickly in badminton to reach the next shot.[1] Quickness training can increase reaction times which are helpful in a fast-paced sport such as badminton.[1] SAQ training is appropriate for small numbers of people with similar goals.[1] Some SAQ drills may replicate the movements and demands of badminton very closely.[1]

Power

Plyometrics

Plyometric training involves **lunging**, **bounding**, **incline press-ups**, **barrier hopping** and **jumping** to develop **power**, **speed** and **explosive strength**. Plyometrics make use of gravity to extend muscles (eccentric contraction) before making a larger concentric contraction. For example, jumping off a box into a deep squat to lengthen the quadriceps before jumping higher onto another box.

Advantages
Suitable for individuals or small groups of people with similar requirements.
Can be performed anywhere with no specialist equipment required.
Simulates many sporting movements such as those in high jump, volleyball sprint starts and javelin throwing.

Disadvantages
Not suitable for beginners or children under 15.
Requires a high level of fitness to start with as there is a high risk of injury.
Repetitive jumping and bounding can cause stress on the joints.

Balance

Balance involves the use of specific training exercises that require balancing on a reduced size base of support.

Sports such as gymnastics, skiing and horse riding require a combination of static (still) and dynamic (whilst moving) balance.

Advantages
Doesn't need to involve specialist equipment, venues or set up.
Can be used to develop specific aspects of balance to replicate elements of different sports.

Disadvantages
Can be restricted by apparatus, space and area, but groups could take part together.
Risk of injury / falling if mats are not used or available.

Coordination

Coordination is improved by doing specific training exercises using two or more body parts together. Sports drills are commonly used to improve coordination for high specificity and to closely replicate the demands of the sport.

Some sports require higher levels of coordination than others. Ball and racket sports, for example involve more coordination than distance running. Training to improve coordination requires very little equipment but can be hard to accurately assess improvements. The wall toss test can be used to measure coordination. See **page 24**.

Reaction time

Reaction time can be improved through the use of specific training exercises to practise quick responses to an external stimulus, for example the BATAK Pro frame, or a football penalty ball launching machine.

Each of the relevant training methods vary in the amount of equipment required, the ease of set up and the degree to which they replicate the demands of the sport. Reaction time tends to need specialist equipment but can be improved quickly with suitable training. Reaction testing can be measured using the ruler drop test. See **page 26**.

2. (a) Define coordination. [1]

   (b) Explain the importance of coordination for a tennis player. [2]

3. Adam is helping a training partner to improve their reaction time out of the blocks in sprinting. On a hand clap signal by Adam, the partner leaves the blocks for a few paces and repeats.

   Give **one** advantage and **one** disadvantage of this fitness training method. [2]

2. (a) The ability to move two or more body parts together smoothly and efficiently.[1]

(b) Hand eye coordination is required when hitting the ball.[1] *The player must align their body with the incoming shot and position themself to strike with power.*[1] *The racket should hit the ball in the sweet spot so that they get maximum power on the ball.*[1] *To hit a ball on the move.*[1] *The player must move into the right position on the court to hit the ball before the ball reaches that point.*[1] *Better coordination should result in more shot points awarded / fewer unforced errors, providing a competitive advantage.*[1] *A serve must be coordinated to toss the ball up and hit it perfectly.*[1]

3. Advantages include: Can be used with more than one training partner.[1] *There is no costly equipment required.*[1] *It is easy to set up.*[1] *Can be done in any location where there is space.*[1] *Specificity in targeting reaction time responses.*[1] *Closely replicates the demands of sprinting.*[1]

Disadvantages include: Require sufficient space for a short sprint.[1] *Participants limited to a small group.*[1] *Could result in injury if not correctly warmed up / if performed incorrectly.*[1]

PROVISION FOR TAKING PART IN FITNESS TRAINING METHODS

The provision of fitness training varies between providers in relation to types of equipment available, cost, other support available and access.

Public provision

Public provision includes schools and local authority (council) run sports centres. It also include community centres, parks and open spaces, and cycle paths.

Advantages

- Available to everybody, including those with specific needs.
- Cheaper with pay-per-visit charges which makes it more affordable.
- Offers classes for a range of different groups, e.g. mothers and toddlers, ladies only swimming classes, or pensioners.
- Provides a social hub for the community.
- Leisure centres are often linked to schools to increase provision, accessibility and opportunity for use.
- More likely to be on major transport routes or in large residential areas which improves access and reduces travel times or distances.

Disadvantages

- Facilities may be basic or tired which may put people off.
- Quality of provision can vary hugely.

The government commonly subsidies sports and leisure centre use which reduces the cost.

Evie is 16 and enjoys hockey in school. She has been encouraged by her teacher to join a local club for more experience and training. Assess the provision options that she may have locally. [6]

Evie could find out if there are any local hockey clubs or teams run by volunteers[✓] in her area. She may also know others that go there so would have familiar faces or friends[✓] in the club straightaway. The coaching at a volunteer-run club may not be as good as a private sports club[✓] may be able to offer, but private clubs may limit their membership[✓] by age, and she may not have the funds to be able to join.[✓] As there are fewer private clubs than public sports centres[✓], and private clubs are often further from public transport links[✓], a private club may be more difficult for her to get to[✓] without getting a lift. A public leisure centre may have training facilities and free or cheap classes[✓] that could help her develop specific components of fitness for hockey. Whilst the facilities are unlikely to be as good as a private club[✓], they may also have pitches that are available for use to all[✓] in the evenings and a hockey class that she could join.[✓] Since there are no requirements to join[✓], she would have no problems attending if there was space in the class.[✓]

This question should be marked in accordance with the levels-based mark scheme on page 59.

Voluntary provision

Voluntary provision involves volunteers to help run local clubs and sports teams in a community. Such clubs are considered the 'grass roots' of UK sport.

Advantages

- Facilities and coaching are commonly free or minimal cost.
- Helps to support underrepresented groups.
- Helps to create a friendly community hub.

Disadvantages

- Level of expertise is generally low.
- Provision depends on the availability and goodwill of volunteers.
- Equipment may be limited, tired or of poorer quality.

Private provision

Private provision of training facilities and tuition is made by profit-making companies and organisations who offer an exclusive service, often for a regular payment. As they are not open to the general public, they may also have membership criteria as well as a regular cost and a joining fee.

Advantages

- Generally, a higher standard of facilities and superior coaching.
- More, and higher-tech equipment which makes it easier to get a turn on a fitness machine and increases motivation.
- Fitness classes may have better availability of classes and greater choice.
- May also offer services such as massage and physiotherapy.
- Exclusive.

Disadvantages

- Expensive compared to other providers so membership cost may be difficult to sustain.
- Membership criteria will exclude some people.
- Location of private facilities may not be very close to home or work.

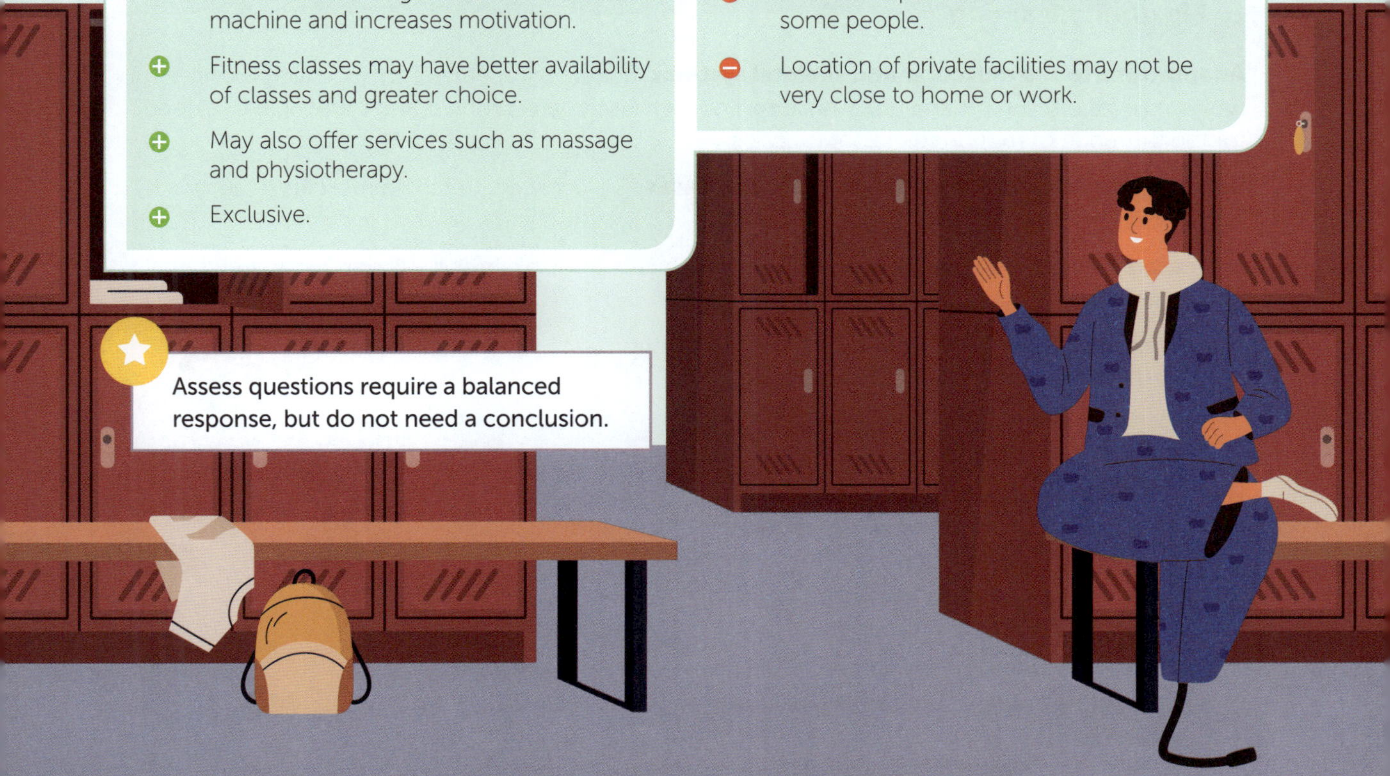

Assess questions require a balanced response, but do not need a conclusion.

THE EFFECTS OF LONG-TERM FITNESS TRAINING ON THE BODY SYSTEMS

Long-term training affects the different body systems, which can lead to adaptations to improve specific components of fitness.

Aerobic endurance training

Adaptations to the cardiovascular and respiratory systems occur as the heart and lungs become larger, stronger and more efficient through regular, sustained exercise.

Cardiac hypertrophy (Increased size and strength of the heart) results in a stronger, healthier heart, reducing the resting heart rate and the risk of heart attacks, angina and coronary heart disease.

Decreased resting heart rate (**bradycardia**) occurs as a healthier, more muscular, heart can circulate a higher volume of blood with each beat, delivering sufficient oxygen to a resting body with greater efficiency.

Increased strength of respiratory muscles such as the diaphragm and external intercostal muscles through hypertrophy improves breathing and lung volume.

Capillarisation is an increase in the number of capillaries as a result of regular exercise over time. The density of capillaries around the **alveoli** increases to facilitate more efficient gas exchange in the lungs.

Flexibility training

Adaptations to the muscular and skeletal systems include reduced tension in resting muscles which relieves discomfort and helps posture. Looser muscles are stronger and more able to extend for the full range of motion than tight muscles.

Range of movement permitted at a joint increases as a result of stretching muscles to allow for freer movement and greater agility.

Increased flexibility of ligaments and tendons occurs through flexibility training and stretching which helps to protect joints and reduce injury.

Increased muscle length increases the range of motion at a joint and the force produced by the muscle.

Weightlifters develop larger muscles over time. Give **one** other long-term effect of training with heavy weights. [1]

One from: Increased tendon and ligament strength.[1] *Increased bone density.*[1] *Capillarisation around muscle tissues.*[1]

Muscular endurance training

Adaptations to the muscular system for endurance helps you perform stronger and for longer. The ability to move your body and muscles repeatedly without fatiguing increases with regular exercise. Greater resistance to fatigue develops as muscles become less tired through greater efficiency of the body to produce energy. This is especially helpful for endurance athletes and games players.

Capillarisation around muscle tissues occurs as the body produces more tiny blood vessels called capillaries around regularly used muscles. This increases the gas exchange to provide more oxygen to the working muscles and to remove waste products (such as lactic acid and carbon dioxide) more quickly.

Increased muscle tone will naturally occur through endurance training around the working muscles without adding bulk. This can lead to a reduction in body fat and weight.

Muscular strength and power training

Adaptations to the muscular and skeletal systems include larger muscles which can increase power and explosive strength in a rugby game for example.

Muscle hypertrophy describes how skeletal muscles increase in size as a result of training or exercise over a sustained period of time. This could provide a competitive advantage over a smaller performer.

Tendon and ligament strength increases through repeated resistance exercises. This can reduce the chance of injury through other training activities or competitive sports.

Bone density increases as muscles pull on them creating more work for them, building their strength and thickness. This increases the protection of a performer's skeletal system and internal organs in contact sports. It also helps to reduce osteoporosis.

Speed training

Adaptations to the muscular system as a result of speed training include an increase in fast twitch muscle fibres and a faster rate of impulses between the nervous system and the muscles.

Increased tolerance to lactic acid means that performers can carry on for longer periods. Lactic acid can also be removed more efficiently through increased cardiac output. An improved rate of recovery enables a performer to be ready for the next match, event or training more quickly.

During anaerobic exercise, e.g. sprinting, the high intensity of the activity doesn't allow the heart and lungs to provide enough oxygen for the muscles to use as they work.

The activity is too intense for delivery to keep up with demand. As a result, muscles are forced to work without enough oxygen and lactic acid is produced as a waste product. The lactic acid causes pain and fatigue so these activities can only be sustained for a short period of time.

EXAMINATION PRACTICE

Topic C: Investigate different fitness training methods

1. Callum is a basketball player representing his local team. He warms up well using stretching techniques and has read that plyometric training could be used to improve his performance.

   (a) Which **one** of the following is a benefit of a warm-up? [1]

   ☐ A – Gradually lowers the pulse

   ☐ B – Increases the range of motion

   ☐ C – Removes lactic acid

   ☐ D –Tightens the muscles

   (b) Warming up has the mental effect of preparing the mind and body for exercise.

   Explain **two** physical effects that can be achieved from warming up prior to exercise. [2]

   (c) Give **three** factors other than stretching and warm-ups that Callum can use to help prevent injury in match play and training. [3]

   (d) Assess the appropriateness of plyometric training for Callum and any other factors he might consider to improve his performance. [6]

2. Rachel is a football player. After years of training and match play, she has been asked to join a new club playing in a higher level league, with a regular income for appearances.

   The effects of exercise depend on the period over which activity is taken.

   (a) Which **one** of the following is a long-term effect of exercise? [1]

   ☐ A – Increased breathing rate

   ☐ B – Increased heart rate

   ☐ C – Improved muscular endurance

   ☐ D – Increased muscle temperature

   (b) Describe **two** ways in which long-term fitness training can improve Rachel's performance. [4]

   Rachel has been training at the club but is also seeking some additional training at a local private sports club.

   (c) Explain why private provision may be more suitable for Rachel. [2]

   Rachel is seeking to improve her speed and muscular endurance. She has asked two coaches to recommend an interval training programme for her.

   (d) Give **one** advantage and **one** disadvantage of interval training. [2]

   (e) Other than speed and muscular endurance, state **one** other component of fitness that Rachel needs as a football player. [1]

The interval training programmes suggested by the two coaches are shown below

(f) Evaluate how appropriate **both** programmes would be for Rachel and make a recommendation about which programme to follow. [6]

Training programme 1	Training programme 2
Warm up for 10 minutes.	Warm up for 10 minutes.
• Run half-mile or mile repeats at a comfortable pace. • Recover by jogging for half the time the rep takes. • Start with a total distance of three miles twice a week, and increase this every two weeks until you're doing five miles of quick running.	• Run for 30 seconds at 75% intensity followed by 30 seconds at 25% intensity. • Repeat for 5 cycles followed by a 1-minute rest. • Perform 5 shuttle sprints of 10m with a sidestep back to the start. • Perform the workout 3 times per week.

3. Laura has committed to train for a triathlon (swim, cycle and run).

(a) Identify **one** relevant component of fitness that Laura should concentrate on improving. [1]

(b) (i) Name **one** type of training that could be used to improve the component of fitness given in part (a). [1]

(ii) Give **two** reasons why this component of fitness is suitable for Laura. [2]

Laura uses free weights as part of her training methods.

(c) Explain how free weights and resistance machines can be used to develop both muscular endurance and muscular strength. [2]

PERSONAL INFORMATION TO AID FITNESS TRAINING PROGRAMME DESIGN

A trainer or coach needs to consider the background and motivating factors of a performer in order to develop a fitness programme that will be safe, effective and best suited to the individual.

Personal information collection

A PAR-Q questionnaire can be used at this stage to help gather some of this information. See **page 11**.

Aims:

The **aims** are what a performer would like to achieve for the selected sport or activity. They may have short-term, medium-term and/or long-term goals. Aims may also be more personal such as to lose 10 kg, or to complete a full marathon.

Attitudes:

It is also helpful to find out about the **state of mind** of the performer and their **personal motivation for training**. The design of a training programme may be influenced by their likes and dislikes in terms of activities, the location and facilities for training, and any particular training methods.

Objectives:

The **objectives** set out how the performer intends to meet their aims using an appropriate component of fitness and method of training.

Lifestyle and physical activity history:

To design a safe and effective training programme, a trainer will need to understand the following:

What **lifestyle** does the performer currently lead? This includes their diet, if they are a smoker, any alcohol consumption, stress levels, and other commitments.

- Their job. What are their time commitments to work? Is it largely desk based (sedentary) or does it involve more **physical activity** such as manual labour.
- What family commitments do they have that may impact time available for training?
- How much sport or activity have they done in the last 6 to 12 months, and at what degree of success and intensity?
- What access to equipment do they have? Do they have access to a gym or sports centre?
- Do they have any current issues (e.g. asthma) or previous injuries?

FITNESS PROGRAMME DESIGN

The most effective fitness programmes should be tailored to the needs of the participants.

Using personal information to aid training programme design

The **aims**, **objectives**, **lifestyle** and **attitudes** of an individual should be used to inform the most appropriate training programme for them; for their goals, their motivation and for their safety.

A fitness test (**pages 14 to 26**) can be carried out before designing a fitness programme to identify a base level of fitness and to provide a comparison of future results. This helps to highlight improvement. A test can also identify strengths and/or weaknesses which helps to set clear goals to work towards.

Applying the FITT principles and additional principles of training

Training methods need to be specific for the participant and the components of fitness that they are seeking to develop. A rugby player, for example, will require strength, agility and power. The exercise sessions also need to get progressively more frequent and intense over time to develop the desired long-term effects of training.

The principles of training are given in more detail on **pages 4 and 5**.

Selecting an appropriate training method

Each individual will require a different set of appropriate training methods or activities as part of a programme **(pages 32 to 41)**. Each training method develops or maintains different components of physical and/or skill-related fitness to fit with the aims and the personal information already gathered on an individual.

Explain how an individual's lifestyle and physical activity may impact the design of a personal fitness programme. [2]

Diet / prior levels of activity / health / injuries / amount of daily activity[1] *will impact the intensity or specificity of a programme.*[1] *Time commitments with family / work may impact the type of training to fit around other arrangements.*[1]

Drawing on more than one related part of the specification in an answer can help you form a better response.

MOTIVATIONAL TECHNIQUES FOR FITNESS PROGRAMMING

Motivation is defined as the internal mechanisms and external stimuli that arouse and direct behaviour. It is the drive to succeed or the desire to achieve something, or to be inspired to do something. This can be intrinsic or extrinsic.

Intrinsic motivation

Intrinsic motivation comes from **within**. This can to lead to continued or sustained effort whilst training.

People are intrinsically motivated if they want to feel a sense of **pride**, **satisfaction**, **accomplishment** or **self-worth**. Achieving a personal best is an intrinsically motivated achievement.

Extrinsic motivation

Extrinsic motivation is driven by **external sources**. These can be tangible or intangible:

- **Tangible factors** include prizes, for example, **certificates**, **trophies**, **medals** or **money**
- **Intangible factors** include the need to perform well to receive **praise**, **feedback** or **applause**.

Striving for gold in the Olympics is an extrinsic factor in motivation.

The benefits of intrinsic and extrinsic motivation on the performer

Intrinsic motivation is generally deemed more effective as it is always within you, and more likely to lead to continued or sustained effort and participation.

Performers can become over-reliant on extrinsic factors. Extrinsic rewards may result in feelings of pride and self-satisfaction, but these feelings may be short-lived. An overuse of extrinsic factors, especially if they aren't achieved, can undermine the strength of your own intrinsic motivation.

Motivation

- Increases participation
- Maintains training and intensity
- Leads to increased fitness
- Improves performance

Explain why someone who is new to training may find intrinsic motivation more valuable than extrinsic motivation. [2]

A beginner may make a lot of mistakes which requires internal motivation to overcome through continued practice.[1] *Intrinsic motivation encourages beginners to play sport for enjoyment rather than for prizes which are less likely to come in the early stages of learning.*[1] */ Extrinsic motivation may fade if rewards are not gained and lead to giving up the sport.*[1]

SETTING PERSONAL GOALS WITH 'SMARTER'

Sporting goals vary according to what the performer wants to achieve. Goals can be set by athletes themselves, or by their coaches.

SMARTER

SMARTER targets are appropriately defined goals that can be used to improve and/or optimise performance. They can motivate performers to achieve exercise goals, provide additional interest to activity, and help adherence to training. Goals can also reduce stress and improve focus.

S Specific

Goals must be specific to the demands of the sport, the muscles or the movements used.

M Measurable

It must be possible to measure whether a goal has been met.

A Achievable

Goals should actually be possible to complete / within capability.

R Realistic

Goals can be achieved given the available time and resources.

T Time-related

A set period of time or deadline by which the goal can and will be achieved.

E Exciting

Goals should be enjoyable to improve motivation to achieve them.

R Recorded

Measurements of progress should be evidenced and measured against.

Goal setting influences motivation by providing direction for a performer's behaviour and by maintaining focus on the task in hand.

Short- and long-term goals

Short-term goals are set over a short period of time, between one day and one month.

Long-term goals are usually set over months or years. They should consider what a performer wants to achieve in the long term, and the best way of doing it.

Nina has set regular targets to improve her golf handicap.

Explain why Nina should review her targets after a set period of time. [2]

To compare actual results with the original targets[1] *which will provide feedback on progress*[1] */ in order to make adaptations to training as required*[1] */ to boost motivation.*[1]

EXAMINATION PRACTICE

Topic D: Investigate fitness programming to improve fitness and sports performance

1. Jo has started playing badminton motivated by the desire to compete for her local club one day.

   (a) Explain what is meant by motivation. [2]

   (b) Which **one** of the following is an intrinsically motivating factor? [1]

   ☐ A – Applause

   ☐ B – Money

   ☐ C – Pride

   ☐ D – Trophies

   (c) Explain **one** reason why it is important to consider Jo's attitudes and personal motivation before designing a training programme. [2]

   Jo's instructor has provided performance goals to help her improve her accuracy and to perfect specific movements in gameplay.

   An unforced error is committed by the player in a situation where they are in full control.

   Jo has collected the following data relating to her unforced errors in recent matches:

Match	1	2	3	Target
Unforced errors	39%	34%	30%	15%

Table 1

   (d) Explain why the instructor has set goals to help motivate Jo. [2]

   Analyse the data in **Table 1**.

   Jo is excited at the prospect of achieving her goal.

   (e) Identify **two** other ways in which Jo can make her target percentage of errors SMARTER. [2]

   (f) Explain **one** way in which goal setting can help to reduce injury. [2]

   Jo has been watching a champion badminton player on social media.

   (g) Assess the effectiveness of intrinsic and extrinsic motivation for an elite performer in sport. [6]

2. Two employees of a courier company are shown in the images below.

Sheena: Bookings coordinator

Adam: Cycle courier

Adam and Sheena are both looking to start a short-term fitness training programme sponsored by their workplace.

(a) Which **one** of the following is an appropriate timescale for a short-term goal? [1]

☐ A – 3 hours

☐ B – 3 weeks

☐ C – 3 months

☐ D – 3 years

(b) Explain how the training programme requirement for Adam and Sheena may differ. [2]

EXAMINATION PRACTICE ANSWERS

Component 3

Topic 1: The importance of fitness for sports performance

1. (a) B – Progressive overload. [1]

   (b) A – Freestyle skiing. [1]

   (c) Ability to make quick changes of direction. [1]

   (d) Flexibility. [1] Increases muscular elasticity which reduces chance of injury / decreases muscle soreness. [1] Limbs have a greater range of movement so they can reach more shots / improve their technique. [1] Flexibility improves balance and mobility, keeping the player responsive / on their feet. [1]

   Cardiovascular endurance. [1] Increases the duration that they are able to perform at their peak for with a raised heart rate. [1] Muscular endurance. [1] Avoids fatigue in muscles used repeatedly throughout a match. [1]

   Speed. [1] Helps a player to reach shots on the other side of the court / aids position between shots to return to the centre of the court. [1] [2]

2. (a) A – Frequency. [1]

   (b) Answer may include: Weights may be increased in the gym / resistance on a rowing machine may be increased / or an incline may be introduced for runners. [2]

   (c) Answer should relate to sitting down / resting. [1]

   (d) 140 BPM. (RPE x 10) [1]

   (e) 220 – 50 = 170 [1]

   (f) 145 / 170 maximal heart rate = 85%. [1] Anaerobic zone. [1] [2]

   (g) Apps / smartwatch. [1]

   (h) Picture A – Coordination. [1] Picture B – Aerobic endurance. [1] [2]

3. This question should be marked in accordance with the levels-based mark scheme on **page 59**.

   Indicative content:

   Gymnasts have excellent balance and flexibility. [✓] Both of these skills are also essential in becoming a successful skier. [✓] Gymnasts are likely to have strong legs from floorwork. [✓] Skiers needs very strong legs [✓] so this may be an advantage as a beginner although more leg training may be required to advance as a skier. [✓] Good coordination of the body parts is also necessary for both sports. [✓] Skiers require a high degree of agility and reaction times [✓] to be able to read the terrain and other obstacles and dodge them at speed. [✓] Gymnasts have less need for agility. [✓] Gymnasts are very powerful, [✓] but this is not so often applied in skiing unless doing jumps. [✓]

   Altogether, the skills required for both sports are very similar. [✓] As a result, it is likely that a good gymnast could successfully transfer their skills to skiing which would give them a big advantage when they first start learning. [✓] [6]

Topic B Investigate fitness testing to determine fitness levels

1. (a) Baseline data sets a benchmark / starting level [1] with which future test data can be compared [1] to show the rate of improvement or regression.[1] [2]

   (b) To design a training programme based on the test results.[1] To determine if training programmes are working.[1] So results can give a performer something to aim for.[1] To provide goal setting aims.[1] [1]

   (c) (i) Illinois agility run test / T test [1], (ii) agility. [1]
   (i) Stork stand test / Y balance test [1], (ii) balance. [1]
   (i) Alternate-hand wall-toss test / stick flip coordination test [1], (ii) coordination. [1]
   (i) Vertical jump test / standing long/broad jump / Margaria-Kalamen power test [1], (ii) power. [1]
   (i) Ruler drop test / online reaction time test [1], (ii) reaction time. [1] [2]

(d) Informed consent form. [1]

(e) C – Dietary information. [1]

(f) To review medical history / to predetermine any potential heart conditions that may make training unsafe. [1]
To assess readiness for safe exercise. [1] To make recommendations for amendments to training or personal exercise programme (PEP) based on any health issues. [1]

(g) Ensure that the test area is correctly measured to ensure the distances are the same as previous and future tests. [✓] Calibrate the measuring tape / stopwatch [✓] to ensure that 20m is exactly 20m / 10 seconds is 10 seconds. Time exactly 10 seconds for the rest stops / use a digital timer with at least tenths or thousands of a second. [✓] Ensure that the surface conditions are the same as every other test. [✓] Allow a warm-up before the test / ensure that she (Andrea) is ready for the test.[✓] Use a standard recording of the beeps. [✓] Use a proper record sheet to record the results rather than using memory. [✓] Andrea should also consider how relevant the yo-yo test is for a hockey player. Yo-yo tests measure aerobic endurance with a start/stop nature, which in this case simulates the sustained action in field hockey games [✓] but this measures physical fitness rather than physical skill such as the Illinois agility test or T test for example. [✓]

This question should be marked in accordance with the levels-based mark scheme on **page 59**. [6]

2. (a) B – Motor racing. [1]

(b) C – Cooper 12-minute run/swim test and the Harvard step test. [1]

(c) (i) Power is explosive strength / the product of strength x speed. [1]

(ii) Examples include: Sprinting to launch out of the blocks and sustain speed / hurdles / boxing to throw a fast, hard punch / shot put to launch the put / volleyball to spike. [1]

(iii) Vertical jump test / standing long/broad jump / Margaria-Kalamen power test. [1]

(d) Kyle's score indicates that he has average agility. [1] Michelle's score indicates that she has good agility. [1] Even though Kyle performed the test faster than Michelle, as a male, he is expected to be faster [1] / the scores compensate for males and females so Michelle is grouped in a higher performance category. [1] [3]

3. (a) Use the handgrip dynamometer in the dominant hand. [1] Squeeze the handle with maximum effort. [1] Keep the elbow at 90 degrees. [1] Keep the arm close to the body. [1] Record the best score. [1] [3]

(b) **Indicative content may include:**

Knowledge of the grip test e.g:

- The test measures grip strength.
- The test does not measure the strength of any other muscle group.
- A rock climber needs strong hands and grip in order to hold on to a rock face.
- A kayaker does not need a very strong grip, other than to hold onto the paddle.
- The test is a standard test to measure grip strength with national benchmarks.

The importance of the test to a rock climber and a kayaker e.g:

- Grip strength is a fundamental skill for rock climbing as climbers need to use hand holds.
- A kayaker needs to be able to hold on to the paddle, but there are far more important muscle groups such as the arms and back that depend more on strength in kayaking.
- The test does, to some extent, replicate the movements of a rock climber using hand holds. It does not replicate the movements of kayaking.
- Grip strength dynamometers may measure grip more in the whole hand rather than just the strength of the fingertips to cling onto a rock, so it may be limited as a measure of climbing ability.
- Grip strength is a poor indicator of ability for a kayaker since it does not evaluate their overall strength, but it may provide some indication of general fitness and strength.
- There are other standardised tests that may be better for both rock climbers and kayakers such as a sit-up bleep test or a wall toss test to measure muscular endurance and coordination

This question should be marked in accordance with the levels-based mark scheme on **page 59**. [6]

Topic C Investigate different fitness training methods

1. (a) B – Increases range of motion. [1]

   (b) Warming up prepares your body for activity by raising pulse / heart rate / speeding up your cardiovascular system. [1] Increased blood flow loosens the joints [1] and provides greater flow of oxygen to the muscles. [1] Mobility exercise and stretching prepares muscles for physical stress and improves the range of movement. [1] [2]

   (c) Three from: Avoid over training [1], wear appropriate clothing and footwear [1], use PPE [1], compete at the appropriate level [1], use the correct technique [1], lift and carry equipment safely [1], cool down properly. [1] [3]

   (d) **Indicative content may include:**

   Knowledge of plyometric training and other factors e.g.

   - Plyometric training involves jumping, bounding and hopping
   - It is good at developing power / explosive strength, but also speed
   - Training involves creating an eccentric contraction of a muscle which moves straight into a larger concentric contraction to maximise the length of the contraction and the power of the muscle movement
   - Diet may improve performance alongside any types of training
   - The principles of training and FITT should be applied, regardless of the type of training
   - Callum should plan his warm-ups, rest periods and recovery.

   Application to Callum e.g.

   - Plyometric training can improve Callum's muscular endurance
   - Plyometric training can improve Callum's power
   - Plyometric training can improve Callum's speed
   - Power will be needed to jump or to avoid or quickly dodge another player
   - Callum will need a high level of fitness before starting plyometric training as it exerts high forces on muscles which could tear if he isn't already strong as there is a high risk of injury
   - If Callum adopts plyometric training during the basketball playing season, an injury could mean he misses the remaining fixtures
   - Callum would not need any specialist equipment and could practice plyometrics almost anywhere
   - The additional principles of training and FITT need to be applied to ensure a safe and effective training program. Overload should be reached but not overdone.
   - Recovery practices should be put into place to reduce delayed onset muscle soreness and prevent injury or tightness.

   Evaluation of the appropriateness of plyometrics and other factors to Callum e.g.

   - Plyometric training is well suited to improving speed and power in the legs which is a desirable attribute in a basketball player.
   - Basketball players need speed when running for/with the ball so increased leg power will improve this fitness component for Callum.
   - Basketball players need explosive power in the legs to be able to respond to potential catches, interceptions or jumping to shoot the ball so more powerful legs will help to improve the power and accuracy of a shot, improve height from a standing jump and improve the speed of response to intercept a ball.

   This question should be marked in accordance with the levels-based mark scheme on **page 59**. [6]

2. (a) C – Improved muscular endurance. [1]

   (b) Responses may include:

   Adaptations to the body and skeleton may occur [1] which may reduce body fat / weight / increase bone density which will help with speed, jumps and lessen the impact on landing. [1]

   Capillarisation around muscle tissues will speed up the healing an recovery process after injury / training / hypertrophy [1] as a dip in fitness may result in a dip in performance scores so a faster rate of recovery would help with more regular training. [1]

   Muscle hypertrophy through strength training [1] will increase muscle mass / muscular strength in the legs to help with explosive power for jumps / kicking. [1]

   Cardiac hypertrophy will result in a stronger, healthier heart [1] which will be more efficient, increasing aerobic endurance. [1] Capillarisation of the alveoli make gas exchange in the lungs more efficient [1], increasing aerobic endurance. [1]

   Suppleness and flexibility through long-term stretching [1] can help agility / increase the range of movement at joints / reduce the chance of injury. [1] [4]

(c) Rachel has a regular income from football so may welcome the exclusivity / privacy [1] and be able to afford the membership fees. [1] A private club may offer better standard of coaching and equipment [1] which would be more suitable for those in higher end sports leagues. [1] The club may also offer sport massage and physiotherapy [1] to improve recovery from injury and training. [1] The club may offer a greater range of fitness classes [1] which could match the specificity requirements / more closely replicate the sporting actions of football. [1] [2]

(d) One advantage from: No essential equipment required. [1] Simple to arrange and set up. [1] Develops aerobic and anaerobic fitness depending on the intensity and type of exercise. [1] Easily adapted as performers improve / or for specific outcomes and fitness components. [1]

One disadvantage from: Hard to keep going when exercise is intense / requires motivation. [1] Suitable for individuals or group fitness training. [1] Need access to a suitable space in which to train. [1] Intensity can cause injuries if not managed correctly / performed within the aerobic or anaerobic thresholds. [2]

(e) One from: agility, [1] aerobic endurance.[1] [1]

(f) **Indicative content may include:**

Programme 1 is of lower intensity than programme 2.[✓] Programme 1 targets aerobic endurance which meets the specificity requirements for one aspect of Rachel's training. [✓] Aerobic endurance is an essential aspect of fitness for a footballer[✓] so programme 1 may be better suited as it concentrates only on this aspect. [✓] Programme 2 targets speed, agility and endurance which better suits the components of fitness required for football. [✓] Running, shuttle sprints and sidestepping more closely replicate the demands of football [✓] than the activities in programme 1. Sprinting and exercises at 75% intensity are likely to build muscle through hypertrophy, [✓] improving Rachel's power,[✓] which is also desirable for football in jumps for headers.[✓] Programme 2 is more likely to develop greater tolerance to lactic acid build up [✓] which can happen in fast-paced sections of a match. [✓] Programme 1 has fewer elements to set up [✓] and could be less likely to cause injury.[✓] Programme 2 may be more engaging, [✓] could be completed in less time [✓] and could be performed in a smaller area. [✓] Overall, I would recommend that Rachel follows programme 2 as it more closely matches the actions of a football game, has good specificity and more variety to reduce boredom. [✓]

This question should be marked in accordance with the levels-based mark scheme on **page 59**. [6]

3. (a) Aerobic endurance. [1]

(b) (i) Continuous training. [1]

(ii) Two from: No specialist equipment required [1] / closely replicates the demands of a long distance running, swimming or cycling [1] / effective at improving aerobic endurance [1] / can be used with all three sporting disciplines of swimming, cycling and running [1] / easy to set up and organise the training [1] / can train with a partner at the same time.[1] [2]

(c) Muscular endurance requires low weight and high reps.[1] Muscular strength requires high weights and low reps. [2]

Topic D Investigate fitness programming to improve fitness and sports performance

1. (a) The internal mechanisms and external stimuli [1] that arouse and direct behaviour. [1] OR The internal drive / desire [1] to succeed / achieve something. [1] [2]

(b) C – Pride. [1]

(c) The design of a training programme may be influenced by Jo's likes and dislikes [1] in terms of activities / the location / the facilities for training / any particular training methods. [1] Motivation such as to play for a team [1] will help to apply the right level and intensity [1] of training / the right training methods to target those long-term fitness goals. [1] [2]

(d) As a beginner, Jo could be demotivated by not having a goal / by unrealistic targets. [1] Jo may be more likely to train/ participate if there are specific goals to achieve. [1] Jo may not be motivated to be the best at this stage, just to be the best she can be. [1] Jo needs to focus on her own skills and fitness. [1] Goals may help Jo to improve her performance. [1] Her own performance goals cannot be affected by others, so they are more likely to be achieved by a beginner. [1] [2]

(e) Achievable – 15% may be too low / difficult to achieve depending on the time frame. [1] Realistic – 15% needs to be achievable given the coaching / practice time available. [1] Time bound – Provide a date by which she must hit the target. [1] Recorded – Jo needs to log all her forced and unforced errors in order to calculate her percentage. [1] The goal is already specific, measurable and exciting. [2]

(f) Achievable goals / goals agreed with a coach / realistic goals [1] are less likely to push performers beyond their maximum causing mental or physical stress. [1] Measurable / realistic goals may provide challenge which motivates performers to use the correct (safe) technique / warm up and cool down properly. [1] [2]

(g) Intrinsic motivation comes from within the performer, so they can always feel a sense of achievement with progress. [✓] Extrinsic factors are likely to be medals in elite championships which create a powerful goal [✓] but they can only be won by very few performers. [✓] The rest need internal motivation to keep pushing / keep going, or to maintain focus in between major championships. [✓] Intrinsic motivation may be used as a tool to reach their extrinsic goal, [✓] but provides a way to keep putting in continued effort every day.[✓] At an elite level, extrinsic factors may be the main motivation left as they have given so much time and effort to reach that goal, so intrinsic factors have less importance. [✓]

This question should be marked in accordance with the levels-based mark scheme on **page 59**. [6]

2. (a) B – 3 weeks. [1]

(b) Adam has an active job so may require a programme with greater intensity.[1] Sheena will likely move less at work as she has a desk job so may require a lighter programme. [1]

Adam is younger [1] than Sheena so may require a more intense training programme [1] than Sheena.

Their gender and/or BMI/diet [1] may be different which can both cause training programmes to vary in design. [1] [2]

LEVELS-BASED MARK SCHEME FOR EXTENDED RESPONSE QUESTIONS

What are extended response questions?

Extended response questions are worth six marks. These questions are likely to have command words such as 'assess' or 'evaluate'. You need to write in continuous **prose** when you answer one of these questions. This means you must write in full sentences (rather than in bullet points), organised into paragraphs if necessary.

You may need to bring together skills, knowledge and understanding from two or more areas of the specification. To gain full marks, your answer needs to be logically organised, with ideas linked to give a sustained line of reasoning.

Example level descriptors

Level descriptors vary depending on the quality of the response. Level 3 is the highest level and Level 1 is the lowest level. No marks are awarded for an answer with no relevant content. The table gives examples of the typical features that examiners are asked to look for in the six-mark questions. Once a level has been determined for an answer, an examiner will justify if the response is at the top, middle or bottom of that mark range to determine a final mark for the question.

Level	Mark	Description
3	5-6	• Demonstrates mostly accurate and thorough/detailed knowledge and understanding. • Most of the points made will be relevant to the context in the question, and there will be clear links. • Displays a well-developed and logical assessment which clearly considers the factors or events and their relative importance, leading to supported judgements.
2	3–4	• Demonstrates some accurate knowledge and understanding, with only minor gaps or omissions. • Some of the points made will be relevant to the context in the question, but the link will not always be clear. • Displays a partially developed assessment which considers some of the factors or events and their relative importance leading to partially supported judgements.
1	2–1	• Demonstrates isolated knowledge and understanding, there will be major gaps or omissions. • Few of the points made will be relevant to the context in the question. • Limited assessment which contains generic assertions rather than considering the factors or events and their relative importance, leading to judgements which are superficial or unsupported.
0	0	No rewardable content.

INDEX

NOTES, DOODLES AND EXAM DATES

Doodles

Exam date